GASPING FOR AIRTIME

JAY MOHR

GASPING FOR AIRTIME

TWO YEARS IN THE TRENCHES OF *Saturday Night Live*

HYPERION NEW YORK

Library of Congress Cataloging-in-Publication Data

Mohr, Jay.
   Gasping for airtime : two years in the trenches of Saturday night live / by Jay Mohr.—1st ed.
      p. cm.
   ISBN 1-4013-0006-5
   1. Saturday night live (Television program)   2. Mohr, Jay.
   I. Title.

PN1992.77.S273M64 2004
791.5'72—dc22

2003057128

Hyperion books are available for special promotions and premiums. For details, contact Michael Rentas, Manager, Inventory and Premium Sales, Hyperion, 77 West 66th Street, 11th floor, New York, New York 10023, or call 212-456-0133.

FIRST EDITION

10 9 8 7 6 5 4 3 2 1

FOR JACKSON

May you one day see how truly beautiful
your mother is.

CONTENTS

ACKNOWLEDGMENTS

I would like to acknowledge everyone at Hyperion for believing in my vision. Jennifer Lang was incredibly supportive early on in the manuscript. She always offered positive reinforcement at a time I could have been easily spooked and scared away, seeing as I had never done this before.

Josh Young is the reason you are reading this book at all. He worked tirelessly to formulate my stream-of-consciousness writing/rambling into a suitable format for mass consumption.

My manager, Barry Katz, was always very encouraging and touching with his input. Thank you, Barry.

Without Lorne Michaels there would be no book. For that matter, there would be a very different me. Thank you, Lorne, for deciding to hire me for the show. When I was last on *The Tonight Show*, I was introduced as a "former cast member on *Saturday Night Live*." I have done almost twenty movies and a dozen television projects, but *Saturday Night Live*, for better or for worse, is the stick by which I am measured. I have zero regrets whatsoever.

The biggest thank-you on earth wouldn't be sufficient for my wife, Nicole. We dated throughout my *SNL* career, and Nicole, you stuck by me in my darkest, craziest times. I'm sorry I didn't call after the earthquake. I was drowning and should have realized that you were land. Thank you for our son. Because of you, I live forever.

—JM

HAPPY HOUR

IT WAS glorious. I was sitting in the back of a restaurant at 2:00 A.M. with Lorne Michaels on my left, Patti Reagan on my right, and the entire cast and crew of *Saturday Night Live* spread out before us. Patti's tits were pushed up to her chin and she was dripping with diamonds. I couldn't help noticing that she had a piece of spinach stuck to her two front teeth, making it appear as if they had been knocked out in a bar fight. She was really drunk and she wasn't saying much, so she was easy to ignore. Lorne, however, was looking typically regal and totally relaxed, and he was treating me like I was his new neighbor in the Hamptons who dropped in for an afternoon cocktail. It was all very pleasant.

I had been off *Saturday Night Live* for nearly a year,

and I certainly hadn't expected to be in this place at this time. But because the show is always the best party in town, I had returned to watch a taping and then dropped by the traditional wrap party. From the moment I walked into 30 Rock earlier that evening, I felt like the prodigal featured player returning home. Access was easier than when I was on the show. Heads nodded, velvet ropes were unhinged, checkpoints were passed. No one had asked for my ID or my special night badge. The feeling was: He's one of us. He's with the show.

John Goodman was the host. Though he had cohosted with Dan Aykroyd during my second season, I had no idea that he knew me from the wallpaper until that night. As he barreled past me in full costume ninety seconds before one of his sketches aired, Goodman stopped in his tracks, did a 180, and faced me. "Jay, how you doing?" he asked. He offered me his giant hand for a quick handshake and then continued his dash to the stage. Man, did I feel like a big shot.

Even the wrap party felt familiar. There were the same three layers of defense. At the bar in the front of the room were the electricians, grips, cue card holders, and interns knocking back drinks. These were the people who worked the hardest during the week. They deserved the bar to themselves. Past the bar were the tables where the cast members sat eating dinner. And in the back of the room were the tables reserved for the producers, the musical guests, the host, and of course, Lorne. But as I drifted through the restaurant, a strange sensation came over me. I felt as if I didn't know anyone, even though I recognized nearly everyone.

I did say hello to a few of the performers who had been on during my two years, like David Spade, Norm Macdonald, and Tim Meadows, but I wasn't about to sit down with them and swap war stories. I wouldn't have known what to say because nothing on the outside ever had any relevance to what happened inside *Saturday Night Live*. Norm was a guy who wouldn't be able to talk his way out of a mental hospital. If most people were committed, they would eventually convince the doctor that a terrible mistake had been made. Not Norm. He would be there the rest of his life, saying things like "I notice I'm wearing a gown" and "So you really want me to pee in that bedpan." Spade was only on the show so he could sleep with models, and what could I possibly say to Tim Meadows? The guy had been on the show so long that his nickname should've been "grandfather clause."

Just as I was feeling as though it might be time to leave, I realized that I had somehow made my way through the restaurant to the producer's corner and was standing directly in front of Lorne's table. My initial thought was to shake his hand, say hello, and be done with the niceties, but Lorne gave me a disarmingly warm greeting and motioned for me to sit down next to him.

Usually Lorne's table was like a receiving line, yet over the next hour almost no one interrupted because we were so obviously deep in conversation. When someone did stop by to offer the proverbial "great show," Lorne would give them a politely dismissive handshake like Ray Liotta in *Goodfellas*. He made it clear that he was talking to me. And we were deep in conversation.

"How are you? How are things?" he was asking me. He seemed to mean it, because he waited to hear my answer and then pressed me for details. I filled him in on my life as Wayne Foxworthy on *The Jeff Foxworthy Show* and talked about auditioning for movies. "That's great," he affirmed. "Movies would be great for you." At one point, he asked me if I was hungry. "You should eat," he said paternally. "You know what's really good here is the penne pasta with rock shrimp."

At first I had felt like I had intruded on Lorne and Patti Reagan. But I soon realized that she was really hammered and Lorne was more interested in talking to me than President Reagan's sloshed daughter. At some point she left.

My conversation with Lorne drifted into relationships and life lessons. "How's Nicole?" Lorne asked, naming my girlfriend without prompting. He told me that every man should have three wives—"one in his twenties, one in his thirties and forties, and one in his fifties, when he knows what he really wants." Lorne had followed that path, and had a son with his third wife.

We were talking as equals—equals of sorts, anyway—because I no longer worked for him. I liked the man more than I ever had—even more than when I was sitting in his office and he told me that I was the future of *Saturday Night Live.*

At 3:00 A.M. we both picked up our coats and walked out together. Just before Lorne stepped into his limo, he turned to me. "It was really good to see you again, Jay," he said. I assured him the feeling was mutual.

As Lorne's car drove away, I began to hail a cab but was stopped by Max, the show's transportation captain. Max had just witnessed Lorne and me parting company. He asked if I was going home, and I told him I was. He motioned for a black Lincoln Town Car to move forward and take me home.

It was the first time I truly felt like I belonged to one of the greatest traditions in television history.

March 20, 1994

Dear Mom and Dad

They say sit tight and pay your dues. But I'm gonna break. Im gonna run. This has been the hardest year of my life. FoR REAL. NO SHIT. It feels good to identify it. The hardest year of my life. All the snot, piss, and shit. "Hey. I'm full. What's that you got? More? okay. Go ahead. Four more shows and thats it! I honestly feel like I did a a tour of duty in Nam. I think the only reason there hasn't been a tell all book written about this place is because no one ever wants to talk about it. I know I don't. It puts me in a bad mood. Everyone asks me the same questions all the time. I wish you two were here in Los-Angeles with the sun and his bullshit. After twenty shows I feel like an old man. (I've only completed sixteen shows as of this writing.) Slowly. That's the pace to legitimacy.

love

Jay

ONE

COMEDY IS TRUTH
THE MOMENT
BEFORE ANTICIPATION

I WAS sitting on a couch all alone in the writers' room feeling like an idiot.

It was my first day at work on *Saturday Night Live* and I was told to arrive at 11:00 A.M. for a meeting with Marci Klein and Michael Shoemaker. Marci was the show's talent booker who functioned like a producer at large, and she had basically hired me. "Shoe" was a long-time producer of the show. The previous night I had gone to bed early in mortal terror of being late. Imagine, here is the greatest job you will *ever* have, and you're the asshole who shows up late. Not me, baby.

My alarm was set for six in the morning. The plan was to get up early, take a steambath, work out, rough out some sketches for the show, and then head uptown to the office. I had a dream that night that all my sketches sucked and I got fired. When my alarm went off at the crack of dawn, I was so grateful to still have the job that I hadn't started that I kneeled next to my bed and thanked God. I spent the rest of my morning racking my brain for better ideas. I went back over my sketches and reassured myself they were fine. Needless to say, the gym and the steam were out. It's probably a bad idea to take a steam while you're hyperventilating anyway.

From the time I left my St. Mark's Place apartment in the East Village, I never touched the ground. Didn't these people on the street know where I was going? If they knew, they would all be looking at me differently. Buying coffee on the way to the subway, I had to fight the urge to blurt out, "I'm on my way to *Saturday Night Live*! I'm the new guy!" I swear I came really close. I figured there would be some jerk who wouldn't believe me. I would have to stand there and explain everything to him and convince him that I wasn't lying, I really was the luckiest guy on earth. After all that, I would be running a little behind, so I kept my mouth shut.

I bought a newspaper to read on the train but I couldn't even see straight, let alone read the *New York Post*. I kept checking my watch to make sure I wasn't running late. With each stop along the way, my breath grew a little shorter. This is a joke, right? Who am I kidding? There is absolutely no conceivable way I belong on *SNL*. They are all going to find me out. I'm a fraud. Someone made a mistake here. Me? "Forty-ninth Street!" Uh-oh. Here we go. I walked up the stairs from the train, and when I reached the top, I first saw it.

Rockefeller Plaza is an impressive piece of architecture. It almost looks like a missile the way it juts defiantly into a menacing skyline. The ice skating rink is directly in front of the main entrance of the building, but it's a story below street level so you can lean over the railing and watch couples skate, which is a nice touch. When you enter the building, the paint on the wall is covered with beautiful yet imposing drawings of Greek gods. These gigantic, muscular men holding entire planets are staring down at you. For some reason, I noticed that they all looked sort of bummed out.

I had arrived at the security desk just before 10:30 A.M. Plenty of time to spare. I gave the security guard my name and told him that I was a new cast member on *Saturday Night Live*. The guard had a thick Caribbean accent, and it was obvious that he didn't really give a shit who I was. He asked me who my contact was. I had never heard that expression before. I had heard, "Who are you going to see?"—but never "Who's your contact?" I muttered the unthinkable: "I don't know." That's one way to get yourself to the back of the line. Tell the guard that you don't even know who your contact is. He told me, the dummy with the backpack and no contact, to wait, and he began chatting up a young lady.

Three minutes later, the guard asked me again who

my contact was. I told him Lorne Michaels. Why fuck around, right? The guard called the receptionist on the seventeenth floor to tell her that I had arrived. She wasn't there.

The guard cradled the phone against his ear for about ten minutes while he checked in about fifty more people. He put the phone down and walked away to help someone else. He didn't say anything to me. At this point, I was becoming panic-stricken. I couldn't remember a single name to give this guy and it was clear I was going nowhere until this guy connected with somebody upstairs. I looked at my watch: 11:05. Later, pal.

I slinked through "Checkpoint Charlie" with the next group of suits. Damn, why didn't I wear a suit? I tried to blend in as best I could, walk-strolling onto the elevator. My backpack was sticking out about a foot behind me, so I leaned up against the railing. I was still about two feet from the door. I was officially in everyone's way. I prayed for the doors to close before the guard arrested me.

The elevator doors whooshed closed, and we began our ascent—the eight suits and the jackass in the back with a two-foot backpack taking up all the room. All the suits were blue. They would stay blue the remainder of my stay on the show. I felt really cool pushing the elevator button for seventeen. I figured they all knew what floor that was and would wonder why I was going there. No one even flinched. I stepped off the elevator at 11:07 A.M. The carpet on the seventeenth floor was also blue.

This was where the writers' offices, the writers' room, reception, and executive producer Lorne Michaels's office were located.

After getting my bearings, I noticed what looked like a reception desk to my right. I walked over to introduce myself to everyone, but found that everyone was no one. I was hit with the funny feeling that I was the only person on the floor. To the best of my knowledge, I was right. So I took a seat on a flower-print couch that looked like it had been flown in from Miami and waited.

At one o'clock, the receptionist arrived. She began setting up her desk and checking her voice mails. I had to pee. I asked her where the bathrooms were and prayed she didn't ask me who my contact was.

Walking down the hallways of the seventeenth floor is impressive and intimidating. The walls are lined with photos from past episodes of the show. Every photo, no matter how tall you are, is at eye level. As I walked toward the bathroom I passed Eddie Murphy, Dan Aykroyd, Mick Jagger, Bill Murray, Martin Short, Adam Sandler, Chris Farley, Dennis Miller—everyone. They were all frozen in time, each a piece of history, a part of the heritage of the show. I walked too far and found myself in an office covered in Christmas decorations—in August. Very decorated and very empty. Good God, I had to pee!

On my way back from the toilet, I backtracked through John Belushi, Gilda Radner, Paul McCartney, and

Madonna. I reached the reception area and sat alone on the flowery couch for another half hour. When the receptionist returned, I told her who I was and that I was supposed to meet with Marci Klein and Michael Shoemaker. She told me that neither one of them would be in until at least three o'clock.

Three?! It's one-thirty, for Christ's sake! I was told that if I liked, I could wait for them on the couch. So I waited.

At around two-thirty, people started trickling in. I recognized a few. Adam Sandler came over and said hi and then went somewhere. Marci Klein never came in that day. Michael Shoemaker came in around four.

Shoemaker introduced himself to me. An Ivy League–looking guy in his forties, he was very pleasant, but as he spoke, I couldn't help but notice that he had a nervous tic. It was really distracting. This guy is giving me the rundown, and I'm staring at his face like an idiot.

As I was talking to Mike Shoemaker, Jim Downey, the show's head writer, walked out of his office. Downey, who had a cherubic Irish look about him, was wearing khakis and a polo shirt, and his toothbrush was in his mouth. Shoemaker attempted to introduce me, but Downey stopped him in midsentence by holding up his index finger and pointing to the toothbrush. He went into the bathroom to brush his teeth. When Downey returned, he said nothing and proceeded to walk back into his office and close the door.

Shoemaker then led me into the writers' room. All the lights were out and there were six cafeteria tables pushed together in a haphazard rectangle to form one big table. Every newspaper in print was lying on this table. That was something I always loved about working at *SNL*. On any given morning I could walk in and pick up the *Dallas Morning News* or the *Washington Post*. I sat on one of the couches at the far end of the writers' room for about twenty minutes, alone with the newspapers.

I would soon learn that my new job would require lots of waiting. As I sat waiting for Jim Downey, the room began to fill up with people. At one point, Shoemaker walked in with a kid who looked a little like Björk and said: "Jay, this is Lew Morton. He's a new writer. You guys are sharing an office." Uh . . . hi. The veteran writers came and went while the new ones sat around on couches and tabletops waiting for instructions.

Dave Attell and Sarah Silverman, two comics I knew from the clubs who were also new to the show, had arrived and taken a seat next to me on the couch. Sarah is from New Hampshire, and she is so "one of the guys" that you forget sometimes how beautiful she is. But when you first meet her, wow, you notice! Sarah and I were both hired as featured performers and writers, but Attell was hired as a writer only. Attell not being hired as a cast member, let alone a featured performer, was a crime.

I had always looked up to Dave as a stand-up, so I was glad that we would being sharing an office. But I also felt a little uncomfortable. I thought Attell was fifty times the comic I was and that he deserved to be on camera, too. He might be the funniest living stand-up comic, and he will perform anytime in front of any mike. Sometimes he'll perform at the Comedy Cellar in Greenwich Village in front of nine people at two-thirty in the morning (his preferred time slot, by the way). Whenever he's onstage, you'll also see other comics, me included, huddled in the back of the room to watch Dave spinning out zingers like "I have this blow-up doll that I fuck all the time, but I fill her up only halfway and I make believe she's a model." Attell was also a chain smoker. He smoked anytime, anyplace. Since I was an utter slob, our office looked like it was under construction in about a week.

We shared the small office meant for one person with Lew Morton and Steve Lookner, two Harvard guys. Whatever the rhythm was on the seventeenth floor, Lookner and Morton picked up on it pretty quickly. They always seemed to know what time to come in, what time to go home, where to hand in sketches, and most important, who to ask for help. All that separated the nonsmoking side from the smoking side was a couch in the middle of the room. Within a couple of weeks, we had smoked them out. I have no idea where they went. One day they were there, the next they were gone. I can't say that I blamed them, but Dave and I were happy for the additional space. Besides, those two Harvard guys were bringing us down with all that goddamn *work* they were doing.

To complicate matters, Dave and Sarah had dated each other and had only just recently broken up. Regardless, the three of us had a strange bond now. We were new. We were ready. We were clueless. And we were all waiting for Jim Downey.

Another hour passed and it was early evening. Finally, Downey arrived. "Downer," as Adam Sandler affectionately called him, was actually a great guy. He had a bit of a belly, and he always seemed to have a smile on his face. Downey had written for *David Letterman,* where, I was told, he had created the Top Ten list, and he had also written for *SNL* in the 1970s. He was harassing some of the guys as they arrived when suddenly I felt a rumbling in the hallway.

Farley was coming!

When I say I felt a rumbling, it's in no way a reference to Chris's weight. Rather, it's a compliment to his presence. Chris Farley was the most beautiful human being I ever met. When you met Chris, you smiled. You had to. For God's sake, it was involuntary.

From the minute Farley walked into the room, the mood changed. "Ahhh, now we're cookin'," Sandler announced.

I stared at Chris and thought about what a dork I would look like if I jumped up from the couch and introduced myself to him. He might have just become my colleague, but I was still a fan. As far as I was concerned, he had reset the bar for funny with the first Motivational Speaker sketch that he and David Spade had done with Christina Applegate, where he hitched up his pants, crossed his eyes, and made her laugh so hard that she had to cover her face with her hair like Cousin It.

Farley and Downey exchanged hugs and then Downey fondly needled Chris. "What have you been doing, Chris? Where have you been? You were supposed to be here." A serious look came across Farley's face and all he could muster was a "huh." "Look at us," Downey prodded. "We're all here. Even the new guy Jay Mohr is here." Downey then pointed at me and said, "Chris, that's Jay Mohr. He's a new writer and featured performer."

Farley looked over at me through a pair of blue-tinted prescription sunglasses. His hair was slicked back and he was wearing a black suit jacket over a starched white shirt. His enormous stomach stretched against an old black belt that held up a pair of blue jeans that hung over a pair of old black combat boots. My first thought was that he looked a little like Jack Nicholson.

He started walking toward me and shouted, "How are ya, young fella?" Then he fake-tripped and landed about a foot in front of me facedown on the floor. Slowly he pulled himself up onto his knees and then buried his face in my crotch and pretended to puke in my lap six or

JAY MOHR

seven times. He sold the puke so hard that even I had to peek to make sure he was just fooling around. Chris looked up at me. His glasses were in my lap. "Oh, man, sorry," he said, wiping his mouth. Not exactly hello.

I looked around and noticed the number of people in the room had doubled. They were all staring at me. No one except for Steve Lookner was laughing. It was very odd. I wasn't sure if they were waiting to see how I would react, or if they were wondering if Chris had actually puked in my lap. I emitted a meek "how ya' doin'," and everyone went back to what they were doing. There was no acknowledgment that a 300-pound guy had just simulated fellatio and vomiting in my lap. Chris rose to his feet and walked away.

Welcome to the big leagues.

A few days after I arrived at 30 Rock, the *SNL* cast and writers went on a three-day retreat together. This is something of a tradition, where everyone circles the wagons a week or two before the show starts and heads up into the mountains for some R&R. In the mornings we would play some golf, swim, and shoot some hoops, and in the afternoon we would all meet for writing sessions. The retreat was in upstate New York at a place called Mohonk Mountain House. I had never heard of Mohonk, and I kept thinking everybody was saying *Mohawk* or *My Hunk*.

Very early on I noticed that everyone mumbled on

the seventeenth floor. No one would look me in the eye or talk to my face either. If someone was walking toward me and I asked him a question, he wouldn't break stride as he answered me. Every conversation I had was with people mumbling something as they blew past me in the hallway. If I asked them what they said, they would shout the same mumble over their shoulder. Everyone seemed to do it to everyone, so I didn't take it personally.

Those who weren't driving their own cars to the retreat were supposed to meet outside the building at noon and ride together on a chartered bus big enough to haul an Alabama church group. At noon, I was still on the N/R subway train. The entire subway ride I knew I was going to miss the bus, miss the trip, and be fired for not having enough class to be on time for my first *SNL* field trip. Since Sarah Silverman and I were neighbors, we took the subway up together so at least we were both doomed.

At 12:10 P.M., I boarded the bus, panic-stricken about being late. It was empty. Sarah and I were the only ones there. No one else showed up for another hour. For a while we wondered if we were even on the right bus. But one by one people started to wander onto the bus. All of them were writers who I had barely met or not met at all. I didn't even know what half of the writers looked like, so it felt a lot like being on a city bus. People you didn't know were getting on and sitting down. No one really spoke, and I wondered if they thought they were on the wrong bus, too. Finally I saw someone I knew: Norm Macdonald.

Slowly and deliberately, Norm lumbered onto the bus. He looked like a cross between death warmed over and a drug addict who had just woken up. Norm stood at the front of the bus for a while and looked out over all of us. He cleared his throat and announced that he had been sick with food poisoning the night before. He provided the name of the restaurant and positively identified the culprit as an avocado. Then he treated us to a blow-by-blow of the havoc that faulty avocado wrecked on his system.

The first sign of trouble, he explained, came when he was crossing the street after leaving the restaurant and started shitting in his pants. He leaned up against a lamppost and puked and shit in the street until he mustered enough strength to hail a cab. He explained that no cabs would pick him up because they thought he was a crackhead puking and shitting in the street.

After Norm had drained his system, a cab stopped and he told the driver to take him to a hospital. When the cabdriver asked him which hospital, he said he didn't know. Unfortunately, Norm had just moved to New York and didn't know the names of any hospitals, so he told the cabbie to take him to the best possible hospital. Apparently, the cabdriver decided to put his kids through college on Norm's dime and drove him all the way up to Harlem. Norm spent the entire ride telling the cabbie that he wasn't a strung-out druggie, he had just eaten a rotten avocado.

When Norm walked into the emergency room, he was ghostly white and shaking, causing the doctors to immediately put him on a gurney. As they wheeled him down the hall, the doctor kept asking Norm what he was on. Norm said that he kept explaining to everybody that he had food poisoning from an avocado. They pumped his stomach, hydrated him with an IV, and then sent him home.

You could certainly say that Norm was a trouper. He had been up all night vomiting in a hospital in Harlem, and he was still on the bus at one o'clock. I was late, but I didn't almost die from eating an avocado. I merely overslept.

Mohonk is a huge, stately manor in the Hudson Valley that reminded me of a cruise ship inside a mansion. As I checked in at the registration desk, I looked around and noticed that the average age there was the day before death. It was like a place where Wilford Brimley and Bea Arthur would go to rent a paddleboat—but then here we came and now Chris Farley was running down the hall with his pants around his ankles and Adam Sandler was whacking his ass with a pool cue from behind while Farley yelled, "Look at me! I'm a horse!"

I was looking forward to becoming one of the guys. I woke up the first morning around 9:00 A.M. and went downstairs to the lobby to hook up with somebody, anybody. It looked like I was the only person in the hotel. I wandered the enormous mansion by myself for an hour, wondering if I was missing an important meeting. It turned out that the people I went up to Mohonk with, specifically the guys I was looking forward to hanging out with, already had their weekends pretty much planned. Spade, Farley, Sandler, and Tim Meadows had gone to play golf. The writers from Harvard went somewhere to do something, and all of the producers had gone somewhere else. Mathematically, it seemed impossible not to at least run into someone from the show that morning, but I didn't.

The next day, I passed Steve Lookner in the mansion and asked him if he wanted to shoot hoops. To my surprise, he accepted. Little did I know, but Lookner was a high school basketball star who had played a lot of intramural hoops at Harvard. The first game we played, he beat me 11–3. The rematch was 11–3. After he schooled me in the third 10–0, I quit. On the final point Lookner threw a move on me and dunked in my face. He wasn't much taller than me, but he could have jumped over the trees if you asked him. I stormed off the court and cursed at him for hustling me. He couldn't believe I was quitting. He offered to spot me some points, which pissed me off even more. I went back to my room and convinced myself I was glad that no one was around and I could be by myself.

Later that night, all the writers and cast members

huddled around a television in one of the banquet rooms to watch the premiere of *Late Night with Conan O'Brien*. Conan had been a writer on *SNL* for several years, and many of the new guys knew him from Harvard. You could tell from the excitement that Conan was popular when he worked on the show.

After Conan's first episode, everyone in the room broke out into applause and started giving out grades. Someone started out by saying, "I'd give him an A minus." Another person gave him a B plus. Someone generously awarded him an A plus. I have been on Conan's show eight times and have always had a wonderful time. I watch the show often and really enjoy it, but I thought the premiere episode was a disaster. To me, Conan looked really overwhelmed and nervous. I didn't laugh at all the jokes like the other guys. I said to no one in particular, "I give him a C." It was definitely the wrong grade. Everyone in the room looked at me cross-eyed as if to say "Who let this guy in?" and then went back to their conversations. That was the first time I noticed that my sense of humor was very different from that of the other writers.

On the way home from My Hunk, I bummed a ride with Dave Attell. Sarah Silverman, who had gotten the flu, rode along with us. For two hours we drove back to the city in silence. When we reached Manhattan, it was raining. We got out of Dave's car at 30 Rock, but couldn't get up to the offices because none of us had our elevator cards yet. Confused, we all stood in the rain for a while. Then we shrugged our shoulders and went our separate ways.

When I arrived at my apartment, my roommate was sitting on the couch reading a book. He asked me how Mohonk was and I told him it was fantastic. I asked him if he watched Conan. "Yeah," he replied. "I'd give him a C."

TWO

DUDE, HOW DID YOU GET ON *SNL*?

IT'S IMPOSSIBLE to say that my lifelong goal was to be a cast member on *Saturday Night Live* because it was unattainable. Julia Sweeney once said that *Saturday Night Live* is "like an uncle you hate paying for all four years at Harvard." Actually, it's more like an uncle who touched you when you were seven, then paid for all four years of Harvard. The upside, however, is that *Saturday Night Live* is a much more precious pedigree. Thousands of students show up every year at the doors of Harvard, but how many people walk through the turnstiles each year at *SNL*? A dozen? How many of that dozen, if any, are new performers? Three? Four? Zero?

Even for the best and most well known comics, the

odds were so great that I never considered being chosen to join the show. If you do the math, the chances are so remote that it is literally unattainable—until it starts becoming attainable. As a comic, you are working toward so many different avenues of success that you aren't even cognizant of some sort of master plan. When you are the emcee at a boathouse in Lake Hopatcong, New Jersey, and you're getting $25 and the middle guy is getting $50 and the next guy $100, you're thinking, let me just get to the middle. If you succeed in clubs, that leads to landing an agent, a spot on *The Tonight Show,* and bigger paydays. You live incrementally; you don't sit around thinking, yep, I'm on my way to *Saturday Night Live.*

But like most comics, I had always watched the show. Truthfully, I thought the original shows in the mid-seventies were overrated, and that the only reason they became so beloved was because they were new to the TV-viewing audience; no one had seen anything like them. Twenty years later, they aren't really that funny. Personally, I never thought the Coneheads or the Blues Brothers were that amazing; I felt they were too obvious. The only exception to the weakness of the early shows is Bill Murray. Regardless of how poorly those early shows aged, Bill Murray was timeless. You could have put him in a show in 1820 and it would have been funny. But the show really caught my attention when Eddie Murphy, Billy Crystal, Martin Short, and Jim Belushi were on in the mid-eighties, because those guys could make anything funny.

Being a comic gives you a small leg up because many *SNL* cast members over the years were from comedy theater or famous improv groups, ranging from John Belushi to Martin Short to Chris Farley. I don't know how noncomics got the job, but as a comic, the formula is quite simple. People who might want to hire you come and watch you perform. They either like you or don't. In that regard, I've always thought comics had it easy. The hard part about comedy is that it's not something that can be taught. A stand-up is a lot like a crackhead. They both know exactly what they want. And they both know exactly how and where to get it.

I was definitely born a comic. By the time I was seventeen, I was lying in bed at night wondering whether my parents would notice if I stole their car to drive to a gig. I never had to mull over the idea of whether I should go to a comedy class. What's the old expression? "Those who can, do. Those who can't, teach." How is a guy with a polka-dot tie going to tell me what's funny? What if he sucks? Even worse, what if he doesn't like the Three Stooges? Keith Richards once said that the first time he heard a Chuck Berry record, his life went from black and white to Technicolor. I felt the same way when I first stood onstage clutching a microphone. I was fifteen years old, and up until that moment, my life certainly had been black and white.

I grew up in the small town of Verona, New Jersey.

Verona is practically Utopia in terms of raising a family. A middle-class town of about 16,000 law-abiding citizens, Verona comes complete with clean streets, grassy backyards, lots of Little League, and a community pool. Unfortunately, when I grew up there, the kids my age were primarily guidos. *Guido* is the term that the Italians of my youth would use to refer to themselves. Translated literally, I think it means "really Italian." I've always had a very fair complexion with blond hair and blue eyes. When I would go to the mall with a couple of pals, they would have their dark hair moussed up and slicked back and gold chains around their necks; they reeked of Drakkar Noir cologne. Problem was, so would I. At one time I even wore an Italian horn around my neck—you know, for the ladies. It's safe to say that I looked a little different from the rest of the pack.

When I gave up on my lifelong dream of being Italian, I began to wear my hair the way I wanted, like a normal kid. I began to wear my own clothes and stopped saying words like "mal*ron*." I threw caution to the wind in my quest to simply be myself. But who the hell was I? I was a comedian. Once I figured out what made me high, I would stop at nothing to get it.

One Saturday morning when I was fifteen, my best friend James Barone (a guido) drove me to Rascals Comedy Club in the bordering town of West Orange. There was an ad on public access television that week that Rascals was searching the country for teenage comedians.

Heck, I lived right down the street. I don't remember much of what I said that day, but I can assure you it was awful. Regardless, I had been given a precious glimpse of Technicolor that day. I couldn't wait to see it again.

After I finished high school, I planned to attend community college, but when I reached the parking lot on enrollment day, I turned the car around. I was going to be a comic, and the only school for that was in the clubs. I continued doing one-nighters—as they are called—earning $25 here and $50 there. Through persistence, I met Barry Katz, who agreed to manage me. I made the rounds of the New York clubs—the Boston Comedy Club, the Comic Strip, the Comedy Cellar, and the now-defunct Village Gate—and soon I was approved to do backup at Catch a Rising Star's Princeton club. Though I was being paid $50 to sit around in case one of the comics on the bill didn't show up, this meant that I would have a chance to become a featured performer there, which paid $500 a night. Forget community college, I was going to Princeton.

My big break came when I auditioned to become an MTV veejay and was hired to host the show *Lip Service,* a lip-synch game show. Instantly, I became more marketable on the college circuit because I now had 600,000 television viewers. I knew I had made it when I was hired to perform at my grandmother's alma mater, a women's college in Denton, Texas, for $750—which represented the entire balance of my checking account. For me, the family connection was huge. I proudly showed my mom the contract—though she was more shocked than sentimental because I was going to be paid $750 to tell jokes.

After thirty episodes, *Lip Service* was canceled, but it gave me a lead item for my résumé. I was soon hired to do a pilot for an ABC sitcom called *Camp Wilder* that costarred Hilary Swank and Jerry O'Connell, which would air for twenty episodes. For the pilot, I was flown to Los Angeles and put up at the Century Park Hotel. I was nineteen, and the room had a minibar. My first afternoon, I sat on my balcony, looking out over the swimming pool and the city of L.A., downing beer after beer, thinking, I will never be more successful than this.

It was official: One Saturday night in July, I was going to have a shot at *SNL*. The audition would be at the Boston Comedy Club in Greenwich Village, which is owned by my longtime manager, Barry Katz. As you might imagine, this is an amazing luxury for a young comic. If you can't get stage time at your manager's comedy club, then you'd better leave the business. But it was hardly the home court advantage for an *SNL* audition.

The Boston Comedy Club isn't exactly a suit-and-tie joint. It's located on the second floor above an Irish pub that has live music. Regularly, you will be onstage and hear "Auld Lang Syne" pumping through the floorboards. The club is also next door to a fire department. Now, I don't think it's asking too much for people to call the fire department in between shows, but like clockwork, every other weekend you could count on being onstage at the exact same time someone called in a three-alarm fire. Off the fire engines would race—if you were lucky—but more likely they would sit in the thick Greenwich Village traffic with their sirens blaring, for once, thank God, drowning out the sounds of "Auld Lang Syne."

The Boston Comedy Club is also a rough room. People in the Village on weekends get really drunk, and some wind up sitting in the room. Slurred heckling ensues, and if you don't have your thick skin and your A game, they will bury you. There are lots of things to do in Manhattan, and they know that you know it. White, black, or Hispanic, young or old, it doesn't matter, they will all sit there with their arms folded, telling each other "This guy better be funny." In short, this is the last room you would choose to have a showcase for *Saturday Night Live*. But it was, in fact, on one particular summer evening in this room that I had mine.

My manager drew up a schedule of eleven comics. I was batting third. Marci Klein, the *SNL* talent coordinator, and a few others from the show were sitting in the back of the room with the dreams of eleven human beings in their beautiful, shiny, *Saturday Night Live* hands. It was about 99 degrees outside; it was also the night that the air conditioner at the Boston Comedy Club broke.

Heat definitely rises. As people got loaded and danced in the pub downstairs, their body heat mixed with the 200 or so people sitting shoulder to shoulder in the comedy club. The room became unbearably hot, and comic after comic performed in front of some very uncomfortable customers. The heat in the room reminded me of when you go into the attic of your house in the summer as a kid. As the mercury rose, Marci Klein and company became increasingly irritated.

I went on third, and the *SNL* group all left immediately after my set. Eight comics busted their chops that night, not realizing that the people they were showcasing for were long gone. They had probably tipped two different cabdrivers by now and were no doubt sipping apple martinis someplace with a powerful air conditioner. They watched three comics that night, and I was one of them. Seriously, what are the odds? They're so tough that when Jim Carrey auditioned long ago, he wasn't picked.

Barry pulled me aside that night after my set and told me that Marci really liked me and wanted to see me again, the next time with Jim Downey and some of the cast and writers. I foresaw a tremendous problem falling asleep that night, so I began to get blissfully shit-faced.

A week later, I showcased again for *Saturday Night Live* at Stand-Up New York on the Upper West Side. I carried a very pessimistic attitude into my second audition, which I convinced myself was realism. I didn't take the

32

showcase very seriously. I figured, Why get my hopes too high for something that was nearly unattainable? I decided that my best bet was to just relax and have fun. What I was really doing was keeping my "monitor" down—a term that Buddy Hackett would use years later to explain the DNA of a comic performance.

I would meet Buddy on the set of the film *Paulie,* and my friendship with him became one of the great treasures of my life. For some reason, Buddy took great pleasure in giving me bits of advice and insights into stand-up comedy. I couldn't think of a better comic to be dispensing advice. Buddy truly believed that stand-up comics were special people—not special in their individual talents, but special in our capacity to provide happiness to others. Buddy also believed we as comics had a brotherhood: We were an amazing circle of people with a responsibility to take the stage and give 100 percent every night to make others' lives brighter. He sure made mine brighter.

One day Buddy asked me what my monitor onstage was. I asked him what a monitor was. A monitor, Hackett explained, was the number of distracting thoughts in your head when you're onstage. Thoughts such as "What's that sound?" "Why is the waitress talking so loud?" and "Why aren't those people laughing?" are all part of the negative and counterproductive side of your monitor. Basically, any thought that inhibits the projection of your natural self is a piece of your monitor.

Buddy's theory was that the first time a comic goes

onstage, his monitor is almost 100. Standing onstage is so foreign and standing in front of a live audience is so frightening that being yourself is the hardest thing to do. Yet in spite of nearly everything in your brain working against you, you still earn applause. Even though you had used less than 1 percent of your natural talent, people still saw a spark in you and wanted you to come back. Buddy went on to explain that as you do more comedy and spend more time onstage, your monitor naturally begins to decrease, and eventually it becomes so small that you can stand onstage and give the audience nothing but your true, funniest self. (Inevitably, I asked Buddy what his monitor was. I assumed, of course, that it would be zero. Buddy replied, "One." "One? Why not zero?" I asked. He then leaned close to me and whispered, "I always figure out where the fire exits are." Then he added, "After that, though, it's 100 percent of 99 percent for the rest of the show!")

At the time of my second showcase for *Saturday Night Live,* my monitor was about ten. I thought about all the other comics on the show, about how they were all wearing their "funny" shirts and had groomed themselves to near perfection for their sets. I figured I would be the guy that didn't primp and iron; I wanted them to see what I looked like before the shower. I went to the gym that night around 8:00 P.M. and showed up at Stand-Up New York around 9:30 P.M. I was wearing a T-shirt and sweatpants and I was still sweating. Sure enough, every other guy there looked like it was class picture day. I ordered a beer and joked around with my roommate Mike DeNicola, a comic from Brooklyn by way of Wisconsin. Mike and I drank beer and hit on girls until I was in the on-deck circle.

My approach was simple. The last time they saw me, I was doing my act. This time I figured I would be less structured and show them a lot of different impressions. I can either do an impression right away or can't do it at all. If I have to work on it, it ain't comin'. I also can't look at myself in the mirror and do an impression. Some guys who do impressions will rehearse them in front of a mirror. They contort their faces and examine the changes they've made. If I look in the mirror to watch one of my own impressions, I can't really see myself. It's useless. I've tried it, and for me, it just complicates everything. I can never figure out how you can tell if you're doing a good impression if you're watching it as someone else.

I took the stage with my three-beer buzz and had one of the best times in my life. I truly did not give a shit. I did Andrew McCarthy, Joe Pesci, Robert De Niro, Arsenio Hall, and Harvey Keitel. When I ran out of impressions, I simply had them all talking to each other. I was improvising nearly everything and the crowd, thankfully, was with me.

The entire time I directed all my energy to the back right-hand side of the room, where I thought I saw Marci Klein and the *SNL* people sitting. I stared them down with all my power. As important as it was for me to show them how funny I was, for some reason it was equally important to me to demonstrate that I wasn't afraid of them. After practically every sentence I would look to the back right-hand corner with an expression that said I found them mildly intriguing. It wasn't until I had been offstage for a few minutes that I discovered that half of the *SNL* cast, along with executive producer Lorne Michaels, was sitting with Marci Klein in the back *left-hand* corner of the room. Nice going. I had just spent the most important twenty minutes of my life staring down a real estate agent from Long Island.

I returned to the bar, perched myself on a stool, and figured that was that. Either they liked me or they didn't. I had a few more beers with the gang and decided to call it a night. When I stepped out onto the sidewalk, there was an enormous white stretch limousine parked at the curb. Marci Klein stood next to it talking to the man, Lorne Michaels. Not wanting to look like a guy hanging around and begging for some validation, I looked away. As I began walking toward Broadway for a cab, Marci called me over. Oh, shit, I thought, I'm drunk!

I walked very carefully toward the two of them. When I was still about ten feet away from them, Lorne extended his hand and said, "That was really excellent." I reached for his hand, thanked him, and tried for a quick getaway. Basically, I was real happy with my set and didn't want to say anything to blow it. After Lorne stepped into the limo, Marci pulled me aside. "You don't understand, Jay, he doesn't say that to anybody!" I thought to myself, Then where the fuck is he going?

The next morning I awoke hungover and started packing some essentials. I was scheduled for a gig at Catawba College in Salisbury, North Carolina, later that evening. I was looking forward to the show because I was working with Anthony Clark, an outstanding comic. Anthony is an old friend who stars in the sitcom *Yes, Dear*. We had met on the comedy circuit in Boston and hit it off quickly. Also, I had been to Catawba College once before and the students there were awesome. They were certainly in for quite a show.

Anthony and I flew together from New York to Charlotte, which was about an hour's drive from the campus. The school put us up in a motel adjacent to the highway. There aren't too many Four Seasons in Salisbury. We both arrived hungry, so after checking in, we made a plan to meet back in the lobby in about an hour to score some local grub. I was going to my room to take a nap; Anthony was going to go for a swim.

The pool at the motel was by no means filthy, but the cleaning net lying beside it was a welcome sight. Anthony grabbed the net and began the process of ridding the pool of every leaf and insect that had fallen into it.

Once in my room, I undressed and crawled under the

blankets for my nap. I found a Cubs baseball game on the television and turned the sound low so I could be lulled to sleep by the voice of Harry Caray. As I was drifting off, the telephone rang. My first thought was that someone in my family must have died. What else could have such importance that I had to be told immediately while lying in bed in a roadside motel in the woods of rural North Carolina?

I answered the phone warily and was relieved that it was my manager, Barry. On the phone with Barry was my agent at the time, Ruthanne Secunda. Barry asked me if they had caught me at a bad time. I told him no and asked him what was up.

Ruthanne spoke next. "You got it," she said, plain and simple as that. I froze. Got what? I knew what she meant, but I needed more description. Barry clarified the situation. "You, my friend," he said, drawing out each word, "are a new cast member of *Saturday Night Live*."

Strangely, I was not immediately elated. Instead, I felt like a school bus had rolled on top of me. I was dazed. I felt as if something very serious had happened, but I couldn't quite quantify it. I asked them if I could call them back so I could phone my parents. When I told my mother and father the news, I cried. But oddly, no real joy. I was absolutely dumbstruck.

I pulled on my jeans and went down to the pool to tell Anthony. I had to tell somebody in person. Anybody. Everybody. When I reached the pool's concrete deck, I saw Anthony, now shirtless, still skimming the pool with the long net. I stood next to him and watched for a while. He didn't say anything, he just kept waving that stupid pole around. At this point, it looked like he was removing molecules because the pool was spotless. But he just kept going. Finally I blurted out, "I just got *Saturday Night Live*." Anthony stopped with the pole and looked up at me for the first time. He was stunned. A minute passed, and he smiled. "Well, there goes that nap," he deadpanned.

Anthony was genuinely happy for me. I was lucky that I wasn't doing the gig with some dickhead who would be jealous. That night, in the most beautiful theater I had ever seen, in front of 2,000 students, I was introduced as the newest cast member of *Saturday Night Live*. Since I had done a show there the prior year, they were juiced. I could feel how happy they were for me. What a show.

THREE

A KNEE IN THE GROIN

I DIDN'T have a single idea in my head. It was my first week on *Saturday Night Live* and Charles Barkley was the host. This wasn't bad; it was terrible. The seemingly impossible had happened: I was actually working on *Saturday Night Live,* filing into executive producer Lorne Michaels's office on Monday, preparing to pitch ideas for sketches for Sir Charles to perform on Saturday. I had none, but I did have a plan.

I noticed a semicircle forming around Lorne's desk and guessed that the pitches would start on one side of the desk and then work their way around the room. To act on my own prediction, I had to quickly decide which side of the desk to stand on. I wanted to be dead last to pitch so I could listen to everyone else's ideas and hope for the light fantastic to strike. It was my only hope.

I picked the right side of Lorne's desk, on the far side of the office. After some aggressive maneuvering, I managed to wedge myself into a position where I would be either second or second to last. Dave Mandel, a writer from Harvard, was on my left, and across the room, leaning against the wall, was David Spade. If Lorne said *David*, I was safe; if it was *Dave*, I was probably going to be axed before I saw any airtime. The office door swung closed and Lorne looked up from his desk. One glance generated instant quiet from the rowdy crowd. After a few seconds of silence, Lorne said, "David . . ."

Whew! With the exception of Dave Mandel, everyone would pitch before me. Think, damn it! I prodded my brain. Concentrating was particularly hard because as I was trying to come up with an idea, people like Al Franken and Adam Sandler were telling the host what they had in mind. That's some pretty difficult stuff to tune out. Even more difficult to ignore was a pitch from Tom Davis, a writer from the highly regarded comedy team of Franken and Davis.

Tom excitedly pitched Charles Barkley doing a Kentucky Fried Chicken commercial. Before he had gone far, Charles interrupted with a frosty "What?" But Tom pressed on about how Charles could tap-dance for spicy chicken, slowing only to refer to his notes. Soon Sandler began laughing, followed closely by Farley. The rest of us were staring at Tom, horrified that he was standing by his idea of Sir Charles peddling chicken. I thought I was off the

42   JAY MOHR

hook. Even if my idea—the one I had not yet conceived—sucked, at least it wouldn't be as bad as Charles Barkley tap-dancing for chicken.

I overheard someone on the floor talking about Barney the Dinosaur's new kids' album. I thought of Barney the Dinosaur. I thought about Charles Barkley. I pictured Barney the Dinosaur and Charles Barkley. The ideas were creeping through the semicircle and looping toward me. Sooner than was comfortable, I was next. Life all comes down to a few moments, and this was one of them. If I didn't pitch something decent, I was a dead man. Then it hit me. Charles Barkley had a Nike commercial out at the time where he played one-on-one basketball with Godzilla. What if Charles Barkley played one-on-one basketball with Barney the Dinosaur!

"Jay?" Lorne said.

I steeled myself and pitched "Barkley vs. Barney," a one-on-one pickup basketball game to the death. Everyone in the room smiled. Sometimes it's just a roll of the dice. All those clubs I worked in all of those cities in all those cornfields, and my entire career seemed to have been determined by which side of the room I was on. No matter now, I had delivered big-time. "Barkley vs. Barney" was chosen as the opening monologue of the show that week—the first show of the nineteenth year of *Saturday Night Live*.

———

Talk about strange. Two days later, at 6:45 A.M., I walked into the gymnasium at Hunter College and saw Barney standing under the boards next to Al Franken. The show must have gotten a great rate on the gym, because for some reason we all had to be there by seven in the morning. I knew why the guy in the purple dinosaur suit was there, but I wasn't exactly sure why Al was. He wasn't in the sketch.

It turned out that the producers had assigned Al Franken to "oversee" the sketch. No one told me this, I gleaned it from his body language. I had naïvely assumed that if I wrote a sketch, my role during filming would be to explain how everything should go creatively. After all, they told me that's why I needed to be there. That's why I went. But I quickly became a spectator to my own sketch.

Putting Al in charge wasn't a bad idea, but I felt that someone should have filled me in on the protocol. Al was from an entirely different generation than most of the cast members. He was a grumpy fellow with a constantly furrowed brow who was fast approaching fifty. Despite the fact that Al was going into his eleventh year on the show, he was still a featured player and not a full cast member. He clearly didn't want a rookie's input on the "Barkley vs. Barney" sketch. From the get-go, Al took over the entire production. I can't say I blame him. I had no idea how to produce a sketch with an entire camera crew and sound guys. Whenever I offered a suggestion, Al would look at me like I just farted.

The first thing I discovered was that my sketch had been rewritten. When I asked Franken why several of the jokes had been removed, he replied that I had gone home and someone had to do the rewrite. True, the night before I had left around midnight, about the time it was clear that "Barkley vs. Barney" wasn't going to be discussed for a few more hours. What was there to talk about, anyway? It's Charles Barkley kicking the shit out of Barney in basketball. The most baffling change was that I had Barkley first charging into Barney, then elbowing the dinosaur in the face, and finally kicking him in the balls. I asked Franken what happened to the progression of basketball violence leading to the knee in the groin. "A knee in the groin isn't funny," Franken told me.

Weeks later, when Emma Thompson hosted the show and Smashing Pumpkins was the musical guest, Al and I had another dustup. Emma Thompson had just broken through in American film, and though I knew who she was, I made the mistake of wandering through the writers' room, a blank on ideas that was causing me to blank on everything, and bothering Franken about it. He was sitting at the writers' table chewing on a pencil. He would go through about three pencils a night with his mouth. I asked Al, "Who is Emma Thompson?" He went ballistic. "Are you fucking kidding me?" He threw his chewed pencil across the room. "She was nominated for a fucking Academy Award!"

I thought he was remarkably angry for such an

innocuous question. Most of the writers were seated at the table with Al and had seen and heard the entire exchange. I was being screamed at like I was a child in front of my coworkers. I looked around to see if anyone was going to tell Al to calm down, but they didn't. I was on my own. I looked at Franken and asked, "Hey, Al, who are Smashing Pumpkins?" Franken turned red and then bluish red. Getting up from the table and storming out of the room, he yelled over his shoulder: "I don't know. But they didn't get nominated for a fucking Academy Award!" Uh, touché, I guess.

Charles Barkley arrived shortly after seven. He was much smaller in person than I had anticipated. He was about six feet five with his high-tops on. I couldn't help thinking that Nirvana's bassist, Krist Novoselic, is taller than Charles Barkley. Al pulled Sir Charles aside and explained to him how the sketch would go. He didn't introduce me, so I introduced myself. I told Charles that I had written the sketch and was new on the show. Charles was a real cool guy. He was very personable and friendly. It was seven in the morning, so in hindsight, I guess he was a peach.

Someone from the school brought out several basketballs and Al, Charles, and I all instinctively started shooting baskets. Now it was officially a great day. I was pulling down rebounds for Charles Barkley and he was getting them for me. I really stink at basketball, but, damn it, I was gonna fake it. I bounced a couple shots off the iron and then moved in for some layups. Charles called for the ball and I dished it to him with a beautiful bounce pass. He threw up a brick. He retrieved the ball, shot, and missed again. And again. And again.

I began counting. Shot after shot, from wherever he was on the floor, he couldn't buy a basket. It made me uncomfortable. Should I be witnessing this? After shot number eight clanged off the back of the rim, Charles explained himself. "I haven't picked up a basketball since the horn sounded in the finals," he said.

Ten shots and still nothing. Eleven went in and out. Twelve was an air ball. Thirteen bounced off the side of the rim. Finally he nailed his fourteenth shot from about twenty feet straight in front of the basket. "Let's go," he said. And with that, Charles didn't miss more than five out of a hundred the rest of the day.

There was a stunt coordinator on the set to make sure the guy in the Barney suit wasn't injured, which was a good thing. I had written the sketch so that Charles beat the snot out of Barney. The action began with Barney guarding Charles one-on-one and Charles cracking the cuddly, lard-ass dinosaur in the face with an elbow. In take after take, Barkley was murdering this poor guy. The stunt coordinator assured Charles that there was a professional stuntman in full padding under that Barney suit. At one point, Charles elbowed the stuntman in the face so hard that the entire Barney head popped off. The thing probably weighed five pounds, and Charles knocked it clean off a guy's head with one shot. Nice.

For the next couple of hours, it was more of the same. Barney getting punched, kicked, cracked in the head—you name it. When we finished, the stuntman peeled off the suit. As he emerged from the costume I could see that he was indeed in full padding. Every inch of his body had some sort of pad on it. He looked like he had just fallen off a motorcycle. He was drenched in sweat and his entire face was covered in scratches and abrasions. He looked like he might start crying. Mental note: Never piss off Charles Barkley.

After we finished shooting the sketch, we all had to go to the offices for the rewrites and rehearsal. Charles was nice enough to invite Al and me to ride with him in his limo back to 30 Rock. He talked about golf the entire trip. The only thing I could have contributed was that I once caddied and had enjoyed *Caddyshack,* so I kept my mouth shut. Besides, because I was the new, unfamiliar face on the show, there was always a pregnant pause after I spoke. The guest host would look at me as if to say, "Sorry, who are you again?"

Though I wasn't going to be performing in any sketches that week, I didn't care. A sketch that I wrote was going on the air, and I was cruising through Manhattan in a stretch limo with Sir Charles. Baby steps.

I had written "Barkley vs. Barney" so that after Charles referred to it at the top of the monologue we could just roll tape. When the sketch was over, Charles would say, "Nirvana is here, so stick around." This would eliminate the traditional monologue, which is usually the least funny part of the show. Perhaps this is because it's written dead last. I'm talking Saturday afternoon. Why this is, I never figured out. Since the show opens with the monologue, logic says it would command some type of priority. It doesn't.

The night of the show, I felt fantastic. It was actually happening. Worst-case scenario, I had written the opening monologue/sketch for the season premiere of *Saturday Night Live*. For the first time since I walked into 30 Rock, I felt like I had really contributed something. With "Barkley vs. Barney" as the monologue, no one would have to sit through a host reading cue cards written an hour before showtime.

As the countdown to the show began, I didn't know where to stand. I figured I should be on the floor watching over my sketch like a parent. That's what I had seen the other writers do during rehearsals. When the show is in progress, there's an organized chaos in the studio. It's an electricity unlike any that I have experienced anywhere else, on any other project. Cameras are flying around the room. Actors are running across the studio to their next setup. All of this is happening around the eighty audience members sitting in chairs on the stage floor. The camera and cable guys have worked there for years and know exactly what they're doing. Intermittently throughout the show, audience members would be asked to stand up from their seats to let a crane or a piece of a wall pass by. I certainly didn't want to be standing someplace where I was responsible for any mishaps, especially since there is no correcting an error in a live show.

The moment arrived. Don Pardo, the NBC announcer, ran down the *Saturday Night Live* cast: "Ellen Cleghorne, Chris Farley, Phil Hartman, Melanie Hutsell, Tim Meadows, Mike Myers, Kevin Nealon, Adam Sandler, Rob Schneider, David Spade, Julia Sweeney . . . and featuring Al Franken, Norm Macdonald, Jay Mohr, Sarah Silverman. Musical guest, Nirvana. And your host, Charles Barkley." He lowered his voice to hit the perfect basso cantinato tone. "Ladies and gentlemen . . . Charles Barkley."

The rest of my life began. I constantly repositioned myself to stay out of the way. I must have moved five times in the first three minutes. When "Barkley vs. Barney" ended, the crowd went bananas and gave the sketch a rousing ovation. Charles waited for the applause to die down. "Stick around, Nirvana is here!" he said.

I was in. A real team player. Everyone had seen what I could do, and I was now on my way to becoming the most famous cast member ever. Undeniably, I thought I was going to be the next Eddie Murphy. There was going to be an applause break the following year when my name appeared in the opening montage. I wasn't being cocky. That's always been my personality as a performer. If people leave my stand-up show and say it was pretty good, this wrecks me. Why would this be any different? After all, out of everyone in the country who auditioned, they hired three new people—and I was one of them.

FOUR

MONDAY, WEDNESDAY, TUESDAY

THE SCHEDULE for putting together *Saturday Night Live* was made back in the seventies when everyone was on coke. For the two years I was on the show, the schedule was the same as it had always been. Problem was, no one did coke and we were expected to keep the same hours.

The fact that a show pieced together in two days has stayed consistently funny for more than twenty-five years is truly amazing, but I never understood why the format had to be so unnecessarily difficult. On top of the strain of working the most bizarre hours I had ever known, there was a vagueness to the entire process that was crippling. Everyone seemed to always be on their way to somewhere else. Every question I ever asked anybody was answered as they walked away from me, and no suggestions were ever offered. I assumed that they simply hated me. That would have been fine, but I think that having been on the show awhile, they were just afraid to stop moving. Also, why slow down your day helping the new guy when you're trying to keep from drowning yourself?

When I started working at *SNL*, I was told to be there on Mondays at 1:00 P.M. A few other guys would be there by then, but as with my first Monday, the majority of people showed up much later. When I was hired, I didn't know how to turn on a computer. While other writers were typing sketches and modeming them to wherever sketches went to be printed, I wrote mine with pencil and paper on a yellow legal pad with horizontal blue stripes and red vertical stripes and then sat around the office with the finished product wondering where to turn in my pages. My Harvard officemates couldn't help me because they handed in their sketches with the push of a button. It took me about three days of roaming the hallways asking everyone I saw, "Where do I hand in my sketch?" before I knew what a production assistant looked like. All of them tried to be helpful, but they were inevitably on the fly, so they'd point in a general direction and mumble something with their backs to me.

Early on, it became clear that my body was not reacting well to my new surroundings. My stomach was always knotted. I never knew what time it was. I stopped looking. The clocks on the wall mocked me. Shapes shifted and sounds came and went. I stopped eating out after Norm Macdonald put the fear of a bad avocado in me. I couldn't sleep, and when I did, it was usually on the couch in my office to the sounds of Dave writing and the smells of Dave chain-smoking. For want of a better expression, I started to feel unsteady. I would wake up each morning with the feeling that something bad was going to happen. All day, I would have to shit with the same intensity of a grade school kid who had just been summoned to the principal's office. As the months dragged, these feelings increased dramatically.

One Monday morning early in the first season, I woke up feeling bizarre. Physically I felt all right, but in my brain something was definitely wrong. Have you ever seen an enormous storm approaching while the sun is still shining? Try to take that visual of thick black clouds rolling in and put it in your subconscious. Everything around me looked and sounded normal, but I had a strange and sinking feeling that it was only a matter of time—a matter of time until what I didn't know.

I took my seat on the N/R—the subway line with the yellow-looking caution sign that heads north and then snakes east underneath Manhattan—and opened up the *New York Post*. As the train lurched forward, I suddenly began to feel like I had to escape. Not escape like get off at the next stop; escape like "Holy shit! The train is on fire!" For some reason I took my pulse: 120. Was I having a heart attack? One more stop, I reassured myself.

At 34th Street, a homeless man boarded the train and

began asking for change. What happened next occurred in slow motion. As the homeless man came closer to me with his cup out, I could feel my heart beating in my head. I started to gnash and grit my teeth. I wanted to kill him. But my homicidal intentions were soon overtaken by the sudden realization that I was about to vomit everywhere onto everybody. I closed my eyes and began to pray. I prayed that I wouldn't die on the N/R train by choking on my own vomit while having a heart attack. My heart felt like a volcano ready to erupt.

I was going to die. There was no doubt about it. I didn't think I was going to die, I knew I was going to die.

I couldn't hear anything, but I saw the subway doors open at the 49th Street stop. My stop. If I could just get out of my seat, I wouldn't have to die on the train. I could die somewhere with a little more dignity—on the subway platform or the sidewalk. I stood up and started to walk off the train. Suddenly I was overwhelmed with a fear of having to go to the bathroom. My next thought was to hurry up and run before the doors closed.

So run I did. I ran from the pole on the N/R train at the 49th Street stop all the way to Rockefeller Plaza. The entire way I was engulfed in absolute terror. The world was ending, or at the very least, mine was.

When I arrived at the *SNL* offices, I took my pulse again. With all the sprinting it had skyrocketed to 200. I ducked into an empty office and reminded myself to stay away from the windows. I lay down on the couch and tried deep breathing to slow my heart rate. I did that until I got up and ran to the bathroom and vomited continuously for an hour.

After throwing up everything that wasn't a permanent part of my insides, I felt better—except for the fact that I had no idea what had just happened to me.

Saturday Night Live is written on Tuesday night. For the most part, every sketch that you've ever seen on the air was written just four days earlier. There's some sketch writing done on Monday after the pitch meeting, but the bulk of the show is Tuesdays, baby. Tuesday is actually the only scheduled day for writing—the only day and all fucking night.

The sketches are read at a roundtable on Wednesday. The ones selected for air are rewritten on Thursday. If the sketch is still alive at that point, it's rehearsed on Friday or Saturday (and then it moves to a Saturday live rehearsal before a studio audience and finally to the live show). That's a whole lot of water for a little bit of boat. In short, there is a day and a half of rehearsal for eight to twelve sketches being readied for live television. With this relatively minuscule amount of time allotted for the writing, rewriting, and rehearsal of sketches, it's a miracle that there's a show at all.

Whenever I would ask Jim Downey when I was supposed to come in on Tuesday, he would respond, "You're paid to be here." Me: "But what time should I come in?" Him: "You're paid to be here." That was it. No more. No less. Of course he was technically right, but it's hard to set your alarm clock to "You're paid to be here." Not wanting to be the one to misinterpret "You're paid to be here," I began waking up earlier and earlier.

At first I showed up for work at 11:00 A.M. Problem was, I was the only one there, and I didn't know what I was doing. What should I write? When I'm done writing it, where do I put the finished product? Where's the dictionary? The earlier I arrived, the more deserted it would be. I would lie on the couch in my office and fume. "Isn't everyone else paid to be here!" I would shout to no one.

Each Tuesday I boarded the subway, terrified that I was running late. I just knew that one day I would arrive at noon and everyone else would be waiting for me—along with a pink slip. Before getting *SNL* I looked at a subway ride as theater of the absurd. But now I would constantly monitor my pulse. How could it register 140 when all I was doing was sitting down on the train? I would take it again and it would be higher. The closer it crept toward 200, the more certain I was that death was imminent.

Soon I began taking my pulse everywhere. Regardless of where I was—in restaurants, in record stores, or even in bed at night, I noticed my pulse would regularly race past 200 and I would feel an odd hitch in my chest. A feeling like I was in trouble. Big trouble. I would lie in my bed at night and imagine it looked like a big asterisk inside my chest, spinning and hot, always trying to push its way out of my body. I didn't wake up with the asterisk every day, but soon enough it reappeared, and I would spend the rest of my waking hours feeling like I had to run out of a burning building.

For months, Tuesdays brought two scenarios of doom: I was either pissed off in my office or panic-stricken that I was still on the train. In an attempt to alleviate the situation, I ignored "You're paid to be here" and began showing up at the same time as everyone else, which believe it or not, was 8:00 P.M. At this point, I realized that the show wasn't really being written on Tuesday, it was *beginning* to be written three hours before Wednesday. This left little time for any extensive creative thought, because the sketches had to be ready for read-through on Wednesdays at 5:00 P.M.

Read-throughs were held in the writers' room. All of the writers and production people who had met in Lorne's office on Monday attended, as well as a dozen or so technical people and other producers, bringing the crowd to around fifty people. Basically, anyone who needed to know what might be on Saturday's show attended so they could plan accordingly. For instance, if every sketch read aloud at read-through had all the characters wearing prosthetics, the makeup department would take note of what they needed.

There was something of a hierarchy to everyone's

position in the room. Sitting at the six cafeteria tables pushed together in the center of the room were Lorne, director Dave Wilson, head writer Jim Downey, the cast members, and a few of the tenured writers. The other writers and nonreading participants sat in a circle around the table. Whoever was left over would form a circle around that circle, and so on. Prior to read-through, every sketch had been printed in the same font and format, spell-checked, and distributed to everyone who would be in the meeting.

Typically, there were about forty sketches. Starting at the top of the distributed stack of sketches, each one would be read aloud with the cast and that week's host reading their assigned parts. Lorne was the narrator. Due to the sheer volume of the material, read-through lasted around three and a half hours, with a short break in the middle.

During my first few weeks on the show, whenever I had an actual idea, I would explain it beat by beat in Lorne's office in front of the entire cast and writers on Monday, but I soon noticed that the ideas I pitched in Lorne's office weren't getting any laughs at read-throughs on Wednesdays. I quickly discovered the simple answer: Everyone had already heard it, so even if the sketch was fall-down funny, when it was read at read-through, people wouldn't laugh; they would simply nod their heads as the memory of the pitch came back to them. Feeling like I was catching on, for the third show, which was hosted by Jeff Goldblum, I wrote and turned in three sketches on Wednesday that I didn't pitch on Monday. Unfortunately, things still didn't go my way.

One of the sketches involved Goldblum playing a father who is a dog. The man has a wife and kids and looks like a dad, but he's really a dog. He walks like a human and talks like one, but he speaks lines of dialogue a dog would say. He would say things like "I know better. I shouldn't have eaten that," and his kids would respond, "That's okay, we still love you, Daddy." Whenever he sat on the couch, his wife would whack him with a newspaper. The idea was that the viewers don't know he's a dog in the beginning, but about a fourth of the way through, it hits them. Kids: "Why did you bring fleas into the house?" Dad: "I didn't mean to. I'm wearing my collar." But about two pages into the read-through, I realized that there weren't two funny lines in the whole thing and it might have been better had I discovered that at the pitch meeting on Monday so I could have avoided embarrassment at read-through.

When read-through was over, the host, Jim Downey, and two or three of the producers would meet with Lorne in his office and begin assembling that week's show. This process was behind closed doors and *not* to be interrupted. After a couple of hours, the cast and writers would be allowed into Lorne's office to see which sketches had been chosen. There was no announcement, you simply looked at the corkboard on Lorne's wall.

On that corkboard was your future. The board had three columns running down it; within those columns was that week's show. Pinned to the top of the first column was a colored index card that read "Cold Open." A few inches under it was a white index card reading "Commercial One." In the middle of the second column was another index card reading "Weekend Update." At the end of the last column was an orange card that read "Good-nights," the ritual of the host, cast, and musical guest standing onstage together bidding the world adieu. The only thing missing from the corkboard were the index cards with the sketches that would be on that week's show.

When the doors to Lorne's office opened, you walked in, hoping that there would be a colored index card on the corkboard with the name of your sketch on it. If your sketch wasn't on the board, it wasn't on the air. Period. If you felt like bitching, there was no one to bitch at except whoever else was in the room with you. And quite frankly, if your sketch was on the board, what did you care if someone else's wasn't?

The times I walked into Lorne's office and spotted an index card with my sketch on it, I experienced a feeling nothing short of euphoria, knowing that what I wrote was going to be on television with me in it! The hallways got a little wider. The show once again became my life's work. Everything was fine.

But as the weeks went by, I began to imagine that the

orange card with "Good-nights" on it was my sketch. Every week it would be there, like a franchise. Most shows, Good-nights was the only time I was on camera—until I stopped showing up for Good-nights.

Things got started on Tuesday nights around 9:00 P.M. With Wednesday's read-through looming, each tick of the clock represented time wasted to me. Instead of writing the show Tuesday mornings and into the evening, everyone was running around panicked that they wouldn't meet this self-imposed deadline. Many of us slept in our offices, if at all. You were always at the mercy of whomever you were writing the sketch with.

After hearing me quote the Christopher Walken/Dennis Hopper scene from the movie *True Romance,* Rob Schneider approached me on my second Monday evening and suggested that we write up a Christopher Walken sketch. I was excited about the collaboration, mostly because Rob knew what the hell he was doing and I didn't. He told me he had three other sketches he was working on, but he definitely wanted to write up a Walken piece on Tuesday once he cleared himself some time.

On Tuesday, Rob showed up for work around midnight. He quickly prioritized the sketches he was writing, and due to the fact that I didn't spot him the minute he arrived and couldn't find him for several more hours, mine was last. At around 3:00 A.M. on Wednesday morning, we began to write. At 5:00 A.M. Rob said he was fighting a cold and needed to go home.

"When will we finish the sketch?" I asked.

"In the morning," he said over his shoulder as he walked to the elevators.

At noon the next day, there was no sign of Rob. I couldn't take it anymore, so I called him at his apartment. He was sleeping—and very pissed that I woke him up. "When are we going to finish the sketch?" I asked. This elicted a long pause, followed by "When I get there." And then he hung up.

I expected him to arrive momentarily. Apparently, however, my wake-up call was successful because Rob returned at three in the afternoon, carrying a large Starbucks coffee. With read-through just two hours away, I was a madman. I ranted and raved. How fucking dare he? Rob seemed rather nonplussed. Before he had finished his coffee, the sketch was finished. Rob then quietly walked me through the hallways to the then mysterious drop-off place for sketches. It was a half hour to read-through and we were in the game.

The sketch was entitled "Psychic Friends Network." Though it didn't generate many laughs at read-through, I wasn't concerned. I knew we had something. I don't think anyone at the table had ever heard a Christopher Walken impression before. After read-through was over, Rob kept assuring me the sketch would get on. I'm sure I annoyed the hell out of him—but I figured the time I had spent watching the sun come up while waiting for him made us even.

After an eternity, Lorne's door swung open. The moment of truth had come. I walked into the office and looked up at the corkboard and there it was. Directly above "Good-nights" was "Psychic Friends Network." Hallelujah!

I rushed to my office to call my parents. With each step, my shoes squeaked "kiss . . . my . . . ass." As quickly as I could, I spread the word to every person I knew: Don't miss this week's show! I told everyone every joke in the sketch. I even read the sketch aloud over the phone to some very patient friends.

That week's host was Shannen Doherty, who played Sean Young in the sketch. The basic premise was that a lot of crazy celebrities you wouldn't want in your head were offering psychic advice. At the time, there were reports of Sean Young doing nutty things, like showing up at *Batman* movie director Joel Schumacher's office dressed in a catsuit in hopes of winning the role. Though Ms. Doherty wasn't crazy about mocking Sean Young, the sketch was rewritten—i.e., shortened—and rehearsed, and the host's hesitancy was pretty much ignored.

As the week progressed from Wednesday's read-through, I started getting uneasy vibes that things weren't going to roll my way—even though no one was verbalizing any warning signs. Nevertheless, the sketch was still in the lineup on Saturday. David Spade was to play Crispin Glover, Tim Meadows was to play Todd Bridges, and wardrobe had made a slinky, sexy catsuit for Miss Doherty. We all performed the sketch at dress rehearsal, which occurs at 8:00 P.M. in front of a live audience. (The audience is then switched before the live show begins at 11:30 P.M.) Upon seeing the catsuit, the crowd whooped it up.

After dress rehearsal, Lorne's office door would be sealed shut again and some sketches would be removed from the corkboard to make sure the show timed out at exactly an hour and a half. When the door to Lorne's office reopened that Saturday night, "Psychic Friends Network" was no longer on the show. I don't know where it went, but it was not on the fucking corkboard.

I found the veteran producer Mike Shoemaker and asked what had happened. Shoe told me that Shannen Doherty was uncomfortable making fun of Sean Young. "Are they friends?" I asked. He told me he didn't think so, and walked away. With only an hour to go before air, there wasn't time for a debate. I couldn't believe it. All Shannen Doherty had to do was say two lines, which she didn't want to do because she was afraid of offending Sean Young. Maybe she was afraid that Sean Young would show up at her house wearing a catsuit.

Not only was my sketch not on the air, I was no longer on the air. I had already asked to be taken out of a courtroom sketch where I played a bailiff with no lines. I would rather not be on camera at all than be on camera doing nothing except standing there like the spear-carrier in the school play. I had called hundreds of people and told them to watch my sketch. Now it was vaporized. I couldn't possibly call them all back at eleven at night and say, "Oops." I certainly wasn't going to beg to be reinstated as a mute bailiff and then call my friends and tell them to tape the show and use their slow-motion VCR replay to see me on it.

To put it mildly, I sulked that entire evening. Every time I made eye contact with Shannen Doherty, I looked at her like I was going to kill her. But it didn't matter. I didn't exist. I sat in my dressing room and watched the show from an armchair.

I decided to make a statement and not go onstage for Good-nights. Not exactly Gandhi's hunger strike, but I somehow had to protest. On my first show, I hadn't been sure whether or not to go onstage for Good-nights. I had written the opening monologue sketch for Charles Barkley, but I wasn't ever on camera. I was standing off to the side while the cast filed onstage during the final commercial. Mike Shoemaker nudged me and said, "Go on!" If he hadn't, I'd probably still be standing there.

The only person who even noticed when I skipped the Good-nights was Shoemaker. When Shoe passed me in the hallway after the show and asked me why I wasn't at Good-nights, I told him I was boycotting. "You should really be there," he said. "It doesn't look good." I basically told him that the fact that I wasn't on the show didn't look too good either. I figured I didn't have enough time to tell him about how humiliating it would have been to stand onstage with everyone in the studio audience—not to mention the friends I had called—staring at me, wondering who I was and what the hell I was doing up there with everyone else who had performed on the show.

That night I went to the wrap party with one mission: to get loaded. I hoped that getting incredibly drunk would alleviate the flow of panic that was constantly and erratically rushing into my body. I would self-medicate! It had to work. If I could just get myself to pass out, I would no longer have to deal with wanting to kill someone until I woke up. The more I drank, the more numb I became.

Amazingly, with next to no motor skills at my disposal, the volcanic churning inside my stomach persisted. Barely able to keep my eyes open, I was acutely aware of the fact that my plan was not working. I was alarmed at my own self-awareness. As I reached new lows of numbness, my self-consciousness was at its peak. My insides felt like I had put a blanket over a kicking horse. This anxiety could be cured only by drinking more. So drink I did. I drank until the sun came up—ironic, considering that the whole point of self-medicating was to pass out.

I don't remember going to sleep that night, but I do remember waking up. It was six o'clock at night the following day when I got out of bed. More significant, it was dark outside. I met some friends for "lunch" that Sunday evening at a restaurant called Coffee Shop. The entire time I sat in the restaurant, I fought the urge to run. From or to what, I didn't know. When our meals arrived, I went into the bathroom and puked. This certainly would be a normal reaction for someone who spent six hours drinking beer and scotch, but I wasn't feeling hungover.

Shortly before throwing up, I became morose over the fact that that day, for the first time in my life, I had not seen daylight. This bothered me greatly. Every day starts with the sun coming up, and I had deprived myself of even that. It didn't feel right. Nothing felt right. You're not supposed to wake up at night. I came out of the restroom and told my friends that I thought I had the flu and needed to go home.

I didn't tell them that I was going to run the entire way.

FIVE

SWIMMING WITH SHARKS

KELSEY GRAMMER has two half brothers who were eaten by sharks. I know this because it was in Kelsey's bio when he hosted the show.

Every Monday when you walked into your office, the biographies of that week's host and musical guest would be on your desk. These were courtesy of the phenomenal research department that works on *Saturday Night Live*. You could walk up to any one of them and say, "I need video of Neil Armstrong walking on the moon," and they would have the tape for you in about three minutes. No matter how obscure your request was, they would find it for you. The research department always made sure that you had every conceivable piece of information on that week's host.

When I first started at *SNL*, I read these bios voraciously. I was looking for an edge. I devoured the host's information looking for ideas. After a while, however, I grew complacent about finding an edge and stopped reading the bios. Well, for some reason I read Kelsey's. Dave Attell read through it as well, and we sat and wondered aloud if that was how they became his *half* brothers. Our mood turned sardonic, and we pondered the odds of two of your family members getting eaten by sharks.

The pitch meeting with the host took place on Monday night, somewhere around eight. The writers and cast would all gather in Lorne's office, along with director Dave Wilson, several producers, and assorted technical personnel to say hello and pitch ideas to that week's host. If that sounds like a lot of people to be huddled in one office, it is.

Lorne's office was by no means elaborate. It was one room with a beautiful wood desk and two old leather chairs. To the left-hand side of the desk was a small bathroom with a shower and hotel-style bathrobes hanging on the wall. Toward the rear of the office was a couch that comfortably seated four people. There were a few pieces of art on the walls alongside some great black-and-white photos of the show. It was a very nice, classy, mellow office. It certainly was an odd choice for him to have thirty-five people stand around and sit on the floor for two hours.

The host would sit in one of the comfy leather chairs;

Jim Downey occupied the other one. The rest of us would form a semicircle around Lorne's desk. People would lean against the wall immediately to the left of the desk next to the bathroom door and then fan out around the walls toward the couch and wrap around to the other side of the desk. If you didn't get there early, you didn't have a shot at the couch. If you weren't on the couch, you either had to lean against the wall, afraid to touch anything, or sit on the floor and stare at the host's crotch for the entire pitch meeting. One by one, the cast and writers would greet the host and pitch their ideas.

After the semicircle of ideas was complete, Lorne turned to Downey for ideas. "Downer" always took his time and really had fun with it. He looked like a guy who derived great pleasure from sitting in an expensive leather chair searching for funny sketches. After Downey was finished, Lorne would always ask the host if he or she had any ideas. Usually, the host would say not really and gracefully defer to the staff. Most of them had never been there, and no matter how famous they were, they were on our turf. Sometimes, however, they brought ideas of their own. Sometimes they would have some great ideas; sometimes they would make fools of themselves. Most fell somewhere in the middle.

Mike Myers once told me a story about Christopher Walken pitching ideas. As the pitches went around the room, Walken sat stone-faced, with an almost angry expression. Idea after idea hit the floor like a bowling ball. Walken didn't budge. After everyone in the room had finished, Lorne asked Walken if he had any ideas of his own. Walken paused to gather his thoughts. "Bear suits are funny. Ape suits as well," he said. Uh, okey-dokey, meeting's over. Let's get cracking on the bear suits and ape suits, people!

John Travolta thought he had some funny ideas. *Thought.* What worked against him was the fact that this particular week was one of the funniest pitch weeks I can remember. Every person in the room was on fire, and Tom Davis refrained from asking him to tap dance for chicken. We pitched him everything from the Sweathogs to *Saturday Night Fever.* At the end, Lorne asked Travolta if there was anything he had on his mind.

Travolta pulled out a yellow legal pad filled with pages of notes. Slowly and methodically, he read us his ideas. At the time, he was coming off *Pulp Fiction,* so he was inarguably the man. We all listened as his ideas just kept pouring out. We sat there for forty-five minutes as he flipped through the pages and giggled at his own pitches. We were trapped. The one that he was most jacked about involved him as a Hasidic private detective, complete with a tallith over long sideburns. Without exception, we all thought it was retarded—though in hindsight, it does sound funny. The problem was the meeting should have been over and we should have been back in our offices, but it wasn't. It was being prolonged by John Travolta.

Sometimes the host could blow you away, which is exactly what Nicole Kidman did when I laid eyes on her. To the point, she is the most beautiful human being I had ever seen. She has these crystal blue eyes. When she looked at you, it was like you were getting laid that night. Of course you weren't, because she came with Tom Cruise, who stood in the back of the room wearing jeans, a peacoat, motorcycle boots, and a Notre Dame cap. Tom didn't say anything. He just blended in until he looked at you and smiled. There was no denying that movie star smile: If the guy pumped gas in South Dakota, he would still be Tom Cruise. In my case, Nicole wasn't a sexual fantasy, anyway; she was someone associated with the show who was looking me in the eye when she talked to me. ("How are you?" she'd say. "I'm good," I'd respond. *How are you?"* Wow!) People who spoke back to me in the office during my first season on the show were the most fascinating people in the world.

When Sally Field hosted, she gave me a shoulder massage at the rewrite table, but that wasn't nearly as exciting as her tearing Ellen Cleghorne a new asshole. Ellen pitched Sally Field her recurring character Zoraida the NBC page. Ellen started off by telling Sally Field about how Michael Jordan had done it. Then she explained some of the things they could do together. Through it all, Sally Field smiled politely and nodded. Then, in front of all of us, she took out a (metaphorical) knife and sliced Ellen up.

After Ellen finished, Sally looked at her coldly and said, "Oh, I know, that's the sketch where you have all the jokes and I just stand there like an idiot and do nothing." Icicles formed on the walls and we all huddled together for warmth. It was, to say the least, a little uncomfortable to hear the host verbally dis one of the cast members. To her credit, Ellen took the high road and gave Sally a pass. Too bad. That could have been the greatest catfight not seen in a Russ Meyer film.

Bob Newhart took issue with a sketch I wrote for him that survived the pitch meeting, but he was a little bit more easygoing about it. When he hosted, I was genuinely excited because I had religiously watched his show growing up. I first saw him that week on Monday afternoon sitting in Marci Klein's office, sipping a scotch. He wasn't drinking per se, he was just chilling with a scotch. Hey, it had to be five o'clock somewhere in the world.

In the sketch I wrote, Newhart played a doctor who was a former pediatrician who diagnosed everything in preschool language. If a patient had a urinary tract infection, he'd say, "It seems like your pee-pee has a boo-boo." After about half a dozen pee-pees and doodees, Newhart deadpanned, "I hope you all, you all realize that you are witnessing the actual . . . the actual . . . end of my career." Everyone laughed. I wasn't angry or disappointed at all. Because it came out of the mouth of Bob Newhart, it was like being knighted.

But there was nothing like being prepared to meet the host, like Dave Attell and I were when Kelsey Grammer was there. In the pitch meeting, Kelsey made it clear to us that he would love to do a James Bond sketch. That week, there were about eleven James Bond sketches at read-through. Apparently, Dave and I were the only two people who had read Kelsey's bio, because in about nine of the eleven Bond sketches, the sketch ended with Kelsey getting eaten by a shark. As if that wasn't horrible enough, in some of the sketches he had to scream things at the shark as it was mauling him. Kelsey, ever the trouper, read through all of them, sometimes yelling things like "Back, you demon of the sea! Stop eating me!"

Dave and I sat next to each other with our faces in our hands, tears running down our cheeks, laughing uncontrollably like idiots at the odds of a guy who lost two family members to shark attacks hosting *Saturday Night Live* and reading aloud sketches in which he gets eaten by a shark.

As everyone left Lorne's office after pitching the host, some of us would mill around and wait to talk to Jim Downey. Getting five minutes of Downey's time was like getting time with the Dalai Lama. The line to Downey's office started early and lasted long. I'm talking hours and hours.

Once you were in Downey's office, you never had his

full attention. His office is like a garage in which you can't fit the car. There's a grill, a couple of tennis rackets, and a stuffed marlin hanging over the door. His desk looked as if it had been hit by an avalanche of sketches, letters, and newspapers. Downey would switch from sorting the papers on his desk to lying down on his couch. He was always moving, never looking you squarely in the eyes.

Downey was like a conglomeration of five different people. From week 1, he would always say to whoever was in the room, "I really want to put Jay in a sketch and make him a teen idol," meaning a Joey Lawrence type with an album who takes himself too seriously. For two years, he would tell me how young and good-looking I was and would repeat: "Jay as a teen idol. That just cracks me up."

He could also be sadistic. Once when I arrived with a sketch that I wanted him to read, he put out his hand and said, "All right, let's have it." Instead of grasping the ten or so pages, he let them lie flat in his hand, and he weighed the pile. Then he handed the sketch back to me and said, "It feels a little long." He asked Rob Schneider for his sketch and he performed the same weighing technique. "That feels just about right," he said. He asked for my sketch again, placed it on his palm, and rendered the final verdict: "Yeah, Jay, that's definitely too long."

Most of the cast would leave the pitch meeting and begin lobbying for support from the writers. This, I learned over time, was invaluable. These were writers. Any help I could get from someone who knew anything about turning an idea into a sketch, I welcomed. A problem I faced was, Who really wants to stay up all night helping the new guy? They all had their own weight to pull, and now you're asking them to help pull yours. So from office to office I would go, literally until the sun came up, searching for help.

Several of the guys synced up naturally. Rob Schneider took Lew Morton under his wing. (Maybe we shouldn't have run Morton out of our office after all.) There just was no one for me to latch on to. It would have been so foreign to say to Dave Attell, "Okay, you be my writer." Dave wanted to become a performer, and to get his sketches on the air, he had to write them for Farley and Sandler. In times of desperation, I did beg him to put me in a couple of his sketches. I'd look at the sketch and say: "See right there where it says Spade. All you have to do is erase it and write Jay."

Writers generally had a knack for certain cast members' voices. Tim Herlihy, for example, would write two sketches a week with Sandler. Like clockwork, at least one of those two would get on. It was maddening and frustrating to watch Sandler because you could stay up all night writing a sketch that you thought was great, and then the producers would tell Sandler at read-through to write a song for Weekend Update. Adam would return ten minutes later with "Left thumb, you're the one, I like you better than my right one," and the crowd would go nuts. He was the guy who, if we were down five runs in the bottom of the ninth, you could tell to grab a bat and put us back in the game. The crowd would applaud no matter what he did.

Equally as funny were the sketches that Fred Wolf would write for Spade and Farley. Fred was born to write for Spade and Farley as a team. (He later wrote the movie *Tommy Boy* for them.) He was also a great writer, period. Fred wrote one of my favorite sketches, which was entitled "How Much Ya Bench?" The sketch centered on a public access show with a bunch of steroid freaks bragging about how much they benched. Emilio Estevez was the host that week, and nearly all the male cast members were in the sketch. We dressed in giant steroid-freak body suits and had prosthetics on our faces to make us look like apes. Our legs were hidden as we knelt in chairs, and there were twiglike mechanical legs rigged under our torsos that contrasted with our steroid-ridden upper bodies. As we spoke to one another, our little legs mechanically kicked back and forth. Fred's added twist was that Spade didn't have mechanical legs because his were already so skinny.

Fred and Herlihy always looked out for me. They would always at least throw me a bone and give me a line or two in their sketches, though they never considered me a principal lead. Other writers had a really hard time just writing my name down on a piece of paper. Fred, who walked around with an unlit cigarette in his mouth, always took care of me. Most of the sketches I had two or three lines in were because Fred had written me into them. I never knew why he didn't use some of the other male cast members for his bit parts, but I wasn't going to try to change his mind.

Herlihy, who had given up a career as a successful lawyer to become a writer, taught me the rules of sketch writing. On the show that Newhart hosted, near the end of my second year, Herlihy sat me down and structured a Ricki Lake sketch. It turned out that there was a whole vocabulary for writing sketches that I had never heard. You don't want to tip the sketch, meaning give away the reason for the sketch in the first thirty seconds so there is no reason to keep watching. The shows in the seventies routinely tipped the sketches—the cast dressing up as bees and doing *The Honeymooners*; the moment you see the bee suit the joke is over. There was also an entire art to revealing the host. If it's The Rock in drag, the question becomes, when do you see that? Him being in the *sketch* isn't the reveal; him being in drag is. You also don't want to make it too jokey, Herlihy explained, or hit it too on the head. You just want to knock out the beats—the jokes— and make it work.

Some of the cast were amazingly self-contained and didn't need much help from anyone. Mike Myers was at the top of that list. I never saw him around the offices for more than twenty minutes after the pitch meeting, let alone watched him go from door to door asking for input. He was a strange bird because he was the model of efficiency. Rhythm, shmythm. The Mike Myers sketch was a science, and he perfected it.

Myers wrote his sketches alone. He knew exactly how they should sound and how long they should be. The sketches were always funny, they made the host funny, and they were often franchise sketches. At no time in my two years did any of his sketches ever need rewriting. He would hand in a "Coffee Talk" sketch and it would be flawless. The Harvard writers in particular really disliked seeing one of his sketches on the table. One night Dave Mandel was reading a "Coffee Talk" sketch full of Yiddish, and he threw up his hands. "I don't even know what any of this means!" Mandel yelled. Duh, that was the whole point. I remember once asking why Myers's sketches even needed to be rewritten. No one responded or even gestured. You can respond to an eye roll or a shrug of the shoulders, but not to a blank stare.

One of the few true collaborations I experienced was when Travolta hosted. The sketch was *"Welcome Back, Kotter* Directed by Quentin Tarantino." The Sweathogs were Travolta as Barbarino; Tim Meadows as Washington; Mike Myers as Kotter; David Spade as Horshack; Sandler as Epstein; Janeane Garofalo as Julie; and I played Mr. Woodman, the principal. Dave Mandel, Al Franken, and I were hammering out the beats late one night in Franken's office and things were clicking. We weren't tipping the sketch or making it too jokey, and it felt great.

Mandel knew *Reservoir Dogs* the best, Franken knew the show, and I know both well enough to round out the beats. All the lines I suggested were good, and they were met with positive reinforcement. Franken would throw his head back, slap his knee, and bellow with laughter. There was a slight hesitancy on my part, thinking that he might just be fucking with me. I didn't know how to react to someone actually liking my ideas. We hammered that sketch out in six hours. That was an evening of quality.

The sketch opened with Myers (as Kotter) asking, "Did I ever tell you about my uncle Sid?" Then it launched into a rendition of "Little Brown Bags," the *Reservoir Dogs* theme song. This was followed by the Sweathogs walking in slow motion to "Little Brown Bags." I enter the room as Mr. Woodman and complain about the noise, at which point they all tie me to a chair and pour gasoline over my head. Travolta then dances toward me with a razor. Just before Travolta cuts off my ear, the door flies open and special guest Steve Buscemi bursts into the room brandishing a gun. The Sweathogs all pull their guns. It's a Mexican standoff. Finally, all the guns go off at once and everyone drops dead.

Mondays quickly became my favorite night of the week because each one brought with it hope and opportunity. I would meet the host, who was usually one of the hottest stars in the country at the time, and afterward the host and a few people from the show would all go out to dinner. After dinner, we would all pile into cabs to go play basketball together. The dinners with the other cast members were when I felt the best. I was one of them. More important, I was one of them in public. It was amazing to sit in a restaurant next to David Spade and across from Chris Farley. Other patrons in the restaurant would point and ask for autographs. Even though no one ever asked for mine, I didn't care. I was with them when they signed their autographs, and I would be with them when they shot their first basket. I would also be with them on Saturday night with the world watching.

Every once in a while, that week's host would come along and play basketball with us. George Clooney was a great player. David Duchovny could hit a jump shot from anywhere on the floor. I basked in these evenings well into the next day, when someone would inevitably ask me, "What did you do last night?" Basketball wasn't really my thing, but it felt great just to be running up and down the court.

When Jason Patric hosted, he arrived in the early afternoon. He had heard that we played basketball and wanted to know if he could play, and if so, where the gym was located. I didn't know which gym we would be playing at yet, so I gave him my phone number and told him to call me at my apartment, where I was going to change

84

clothes after the pitch meeting. When I walked in, the message light on my answering machine was blinking. I hit play and listened to a message from Jason Patric telling me he wasn't going to be able to make it because he was exhausted from flying to New York and needed some sleep. I saved the message and played it like I had never heard it before when my roommate got home.

Saturdays should have been my favorite night of the week. Unlike Monday nights, when the building was pretty much empty by the time you got to work, Saturday nights were packed. *Saturday Night Live* was and still is the greatest show in town, and the hallways would be crowded with people who knew they were lucky to be in the way. A lot of celebrities came to the show, too. It wasn't uncommon to be rushing from your dressing room to the stage and pass Anthony Kiedis from the Red Hot Chili Peppers or Charlize Theron or Paul Simon.

And Saturdays *were* my favorite nights—if I had a sketch on the air. If you weren't in anything, you spent all of Saturday night in your dressing room watching everyone else have a great time. But if you had a sketch on the air, everything was perfect. Even if your sketch bombed, you were still accounted for. You had contributed to the history of the show. You could stand onstage during Good-nights and wave and shake hands and not feel like a phony.

Too often, however, I was not accounted for.

———

Even eating takeout with the others became difficult. Food was always delivered to the seventeenth floor, usually very late at night. It was free, so no one really cared what it was. We just devoured it—except for Rob Schneider and writer Ian Maxtone-Graham, who never touched the food the rest of us ate. Ian would roam the hallways with his nuts and yogurt, and Rob would always order up sushi.

Every time Rob received a sushi delivery he would scrabble through his desk and take out a loupe like a jeweler preparing to examine a diamond. He would hold each piece of sushi up to the light and inspect it through the loupe. When I asked him what he was doing, he told me he was checking for worms. He would put the loupe in his eye as if he were staring at the Hope diamond. It was raw fish. "Here's one!" he'd shout. He would hand me the loupe and I would go through the same jeweler motions he did and take a peek. Sure enough, I could make out tiny dots in the center of the sushi. This happened once a week. He told me that you always have to check sushi for worms because they were very common in Manhattan. Personally, I would have stopped ordering sushi, but not Rob. He ordered and inspected it every week.

With the Harvard guys, it was never pizza. It was "We're ordering Portuguese, what do you want?" I didn't even know what Portuguese food was. I would study the menu and it would be chicken followed by a Portuguese word and rice. The next night, someone would announce they were ordering Serbian food. Again, I'd ask for the menu and their eyes would roll, as if they were saying, "Jesus, Jay, don't you know anything?" The first time they ordered Indian food, I remember thinking the second that it hit the plate that it smelled identical to the inside of a taxicab. Being a New Yorker, I was reluctant to eat the smell of another man. I put on a stiff upper lip and ate the lamb vindaloo. When I finished, I looked at my plate and saw that it was stained orange. I went to the men's room and tried to clean it with the grainy, sandy soap. No matter how hard I scrubbed, the plate remained orange. It was then that I concluded anything that stains a plate so drastically is also staining my esophagus and my stomach.

Soon, every time I saw pizza boxes in the writers' room, I would help myself to four slices, eat one, and stash the others in my office drawer for the inevitable night of Serbian deli takeout. Even with the food, I was out of the loop.

SIX

PLAYING WELL
WITH OTHERS

SURPRISINGLY, THERE weren't many fistfights while I was on the show. Tempers flared and people screamed at each other, but for the most part, there were no brawls. The one fight I remember was one between Norm Macdonald and Ian Maxtone-Graham.

Ian was a writer who had graduated from Brown University. Jim Downey used to kid him about it. There were so many Harvard guys around (Downey included) that when Ian suggested something during rewrites, Downey would say, "Is that how they would write it at Brown, Ian?" or "Would that be the Brown version?"

Ian was always nice to me. He looked like a character out of *The Great Gatsby*. He wore scholarly glasses and even sported an ascot from time to time. He was very tall and rail thin. Whenever he entered a room, he was usually eating yogurt with nuts in it. He didn't drink or smoke, and he came off as a bit of a square. Ian's pet peeve was smoking. He was extremely vocal about his displeasure with people who smoked in the building.

The entire building was a nonsmoking building, but that was pretty much ignored on the seventeenth floor. A lot of *SNL* people smoked, and they weren't about to wait for a night elevator to go downstairs and outside to have a butt. Oddly, there were no ashtrays on the seventeenth floor. Because of all the smokers in the history of the show, you would think that someone would've thought to bring up an ashtray.

Since most of the trash cans were filled with paper, tossing your butt in the garbage was not an option. Dave Attell and Norm both weren't bothered by the lack of places to put a cigarette. Whenever either would put a cigarette down, he would stand it up on the filter end and leave it on the desk or table. If he didn't touch it again, the cigarette would burn down to the filter and go out by itself. Sometimes I would walk into my office in the morning and find Dave asleep on the couch. Across his desk would be a line of cigarettes. Some he had forgotten about and left there, because there would be a long line of ash on the desk next to them. It looked like a little graveyard.

One Thursday evening during rewrites, Norm was sitting on the couch by the door inside the writers' room.

He was smoking and ashing into a soda can. Ian Maxtone-Graham walked into the room holding a cup of water. He stopped, looked down at Norm, and poured the entire cup of water over Norm's head. Shocked, Norm sat there soaking wet.

The room grew quiet and then Norm stood up and punched Ian in the face. He really blasted him. All six feet eight inches of Ian went down, and the writers quickly jumped up and separated the two. Ian went home right after the fight and didn't come back to work for about a week. I don't know if it was pride or principle, but my man was AWOL. I found out a few days later that Ian was planning to sue NBC for not enforcing the nonsmoking policy. He was also going to take Norm to court for assault and battery.

A few days passed and word filtered in from the outside that Ian was doing well, wasn't going to sue anybody, and would soon be returning to work.

Rob Schneider was a sketch machine while I was there. He could also be an asshole, and for a long time I really wanted to beat the shit out of him. Only he and Ellen Cleghorne were assholes to me on a constant basis. Ellen was easier to deal with because you didn't really have to deal with her. She was angry at you all the time. If you passed Ellen in the hallway, you didn't even bother to say hi. She hated you and you both knew it. She was a single mom (with a beautiful young daughter) and you were a speck on the radar. No problem. The consistency of her behavior was comforting, almost like a black guy being comfortable with a KKK member because he knows exactly where he stands, as opposed to the Orange County guy who calls him pal in his living room and then firebombs his car. Rob, however, was a much more complex asshole.

Rob enjoyed dressing the new guys down in front of everyone. He would always call me rookie in front of the other writers. I was always more confused than upset because half of the writers were rookies, too. I don't mind a little hazing, but after a while it got real old. The cycle of asshole would start with Schneider chiding me as a rookie in front of everyone and then proceeding to treat me like garbage for two weeks straight. Then, for some bizarre reason, he would wander into my office and start massaging my shoulders and ask, "How have you been, man?" With Ellen you always knew where you stood— out of her way. With Rob, you never knew which guy was showing up.

Schneider and Spade almost fought once. I don't know what the issue was, but for about a week Rob was walking around the offices saying: "Spade wants to kick my ass! What the fuck is his problem?" We all found it quite comical. The two smallest guys ever to be on the show were gearing up for a schoolyard fistfight. After a while, that died down, too.

Despite our differences, Rob was one of the few writers or cast members who really went out of their way to help me. Strange but true. (There's no possible way that Christopher Walken doing "Psychic Friends Network" would have made it on the air on the show Jeff Goldblum hosted without Rob's help.) Once Rob stopped acting like an asshole and encouraged me to put together a musket sketch based on a real-life shopping trip of mine. I had gone to an antiques store to buy a musket to hang over my fireplace. The musket salesman told me the gun still worked. When I explained that I didn't have a license, the guy told me that I didn't need one because the firearm was an antique. Then I started thinking, How would you feel if you got mugged by a guy with a musket? Imagine you are jogging on a trail in the woods and a guy jumps out of a bush with a musket and tells you not to move. Methodically he begins packing the powder into the gun—warning you, as he toils away, to remain still. The punch line of the sketch would be that once he shoots, you are too far away for him to hit you anyway.

Rob and I wrote up a three-page sketch about two Revolutionary War soldiers who couldn't get their muskets loaded fast enough and ended up being blown to bits. The sketch never made it on the air, but I use the musket story in my stand-up to this day.

Another time Rob and I were in his office writing and I suggested we put Al Franken in the sketch. Rob cautioned me, "You don't want to do that." When I asked why not, he led me out of his office and down the hall. We passed photo after photo as Rob ran his finger along the wall so he wouldn't miss the one he was looking for. Finally we came to a photo from 1976. It was a photo of the sketch where Garrett Morris is having a white sale. In the photograph you see Belushi, standing with his gut out. Bill Murray is off to the side, looking like the least desirable white guy you could buy. In the middle of the picture stood Al Franken. His chest was pushed out and he had a look on his face like he was taking a dump. Rob pointed to Al in the photo, said, "That's why," and walked away.

Rob Schneider, my antihero.

Adam Sandler and I almost came to blows once. He had written a sketch where he played Steven Tyler of Aerosmith and I was guitarist Joe Perry. The sketch had just the two of us, and I was excited that he had invited me to be in it. In my early days, I had asked Adam if he'd take me under his wing. "Nah, you don't want to be under there," he told me. "It's stinky." I guess it was smelling better now because I was his first choice for his parody of Aerosmith's greatest hits. The joke was that all the songs sounded the same. As Adam sang each song, it became clear that the guitar sound never changed. The sad part was that it was true.

When I asked *SNL* bandleader G. E. Smith how much

of the sketch was false, he told me none of it. He pulled me into his office, picked up a guitar, and started strumming. He told me to watch his left hand on the neck of the guitar. He swore he could play fifteen Aerosmith songs and never move a finger. I didn't believe him until he launched into "Cryin'," then "Crazy," without changing the position of any of his fingers on the fret. He put together a quick medley of Aerosmith songs to prove his point. He was right. Through five different hits, his hand never budged.

In a way, I resented Sandler. Not Adam the person, but the audience's familiarity with Adam. I felt that if I could just get on the air more often, people would become familiar with me and look forward to a sketch I was in. Having an audience know who you are as a performer is an amazing freedom. It's true of stand-up comedy. When you reach the status of headliner, doing stand-up becomes easier. You don't have to worry about winning everyone over. You are the reason everyone has assembled. Hundreds of people have gathered in a room because they already like your sense of humor. With this, your audience becomes much more patient. They are far more willing to climb out on a wire with you. On *Saturday Night Live,* I had the same audience rapport as an open-mike comic. They didn't know who I was, so whenever I was onstage I felt a sense of urgency to prove to everyone that I was funny.

Even when I was doing a killer sketch, I always felt

like the audience was wondering who was under the prosthetic. When I played Don Rickles, my entire face was covered. I was in the makeup chair for three hours. I had a bald cap on and they fitted me with big jowls and made me new lips. I was unrecognizable. While in the makeup, I walked around the hallways and no one knew who I was. Everyone thought I was an old man in a tuxedo walking around. I walked up behind my manager and told him to get out of my way as Rickles. When he turned around, he apologized and stepped aside. I should have gone out and robbed banks with that makeup on.

I played Don Rickles in a sketch about NFL football moving to Fox. The premise of the sketch was that Fox was using all of its different television stars doing commentary for the game. Rickles and Richard Lewis, played by Adam Sandler, were in a Fox sitcom at the time. Chris Farley played John Madden, who tossed to Rickles and Lewis via satellite. Sandler did a pretty good Richard Lewis, but I still think my Rickles was perfect. When I spoke in the sketch, no one even giggled. They didn't know who I was. They really had no idea, and spent every moment of every line I had trying to place me. I again overheard people in the audience whispering things like "Is that Spade?" and "No! I bet it's Mike Myers!" Sorry, folks, but it's me, Jay, and if you would just give me your undivided attention for a few minutes I will blow your balls off with this impression I'm doing over here. The sketch went over well and got its share of laughs. Just not when I spoke.

During a commercial break, Sandler and I were standing under the bleachers in the studio waiting to go onstage. I had shaved my chest to look more like Joe Perry. I was wearing leather pants and a cool wig with long curly hair, and I had a guitar slung around my neck. Sandler was dressed just like Steven Tyler. His wig was perfect and his clothes were right on the money—except that he was wearing a pair of sunglasses that looked like Elton John's. I told him before we walked under the bleachers that I thought the sunglasses were wrong, but he disagreed. With about thirty seconds left in the commercial break, I tried again, telling him that he should get a better pair of sunglasses. He glared at me.

"Why don't you shut the fuck up!" Adam yelled.

I was stunned. Looking back, I realize my timing was inappropriate. Since he had written the sketch for himself and was gracious enough to include me, what the hell did I care what kind of sunglasses he had on? But I did care. For some reason I cared a lot. I looked Sandler in the eye to see if he was serious. He was.

Then I looked up and noticed we were standing a few feet in front of the overhang of the bleachers. About twenty audience members were reaching over the railing, desperately trying to touch Sandler. I wanted to hit him or at least shout back, but I couldn't help but feel forty eyes on me—twenty people who if they saw Adam Sandler and a guy in a curly wig in a fistfight would dive out of the bleachers and kick the shit out of me.

The worst part for me was that they all saw the entire

exchange. I must have looked like a real asshole telling Adam Sandler to change his sunglasses. There wasn't time to think of a response because we were soon whisked onto the stage for the sketch. We performed the sketch and it killed.

As we walked off the stage, Sandler came up to me. "We're good," he said. "Respect."

He didn't apologize and neither did I. We didn't have to. Respect.

Chris Farley and I wrestled three times when I was on the show. All three matches were on the same night.

The first match happened in the graphics room, which was located halfway between Lorne's office and the writers' room. The graphics room was a great place to go if you didn't want anyone to bother you. When you were tired of the phone calls and sick of people popping into your office, you could always find places such as the graphics room where no one would even think to look for you. Fred Wolf, David Spade, Chris Farley, and I were in there shooting the shit and kicking some ideas around for sketches. Mostly they came up with ideas and I stood there and watched. I had run out of ideas long ago, but I knew if I hung around I might wind up in something by accident.

Somehow the conversation turned to the subject of wrestling. I had wrestled in high school, and Fred and I had talked earlier in the year about possibly doing a high school wrestling sketch. We ran the idea by Jim Downey, but nothing ever came of it. Fred suggested to Chris that despite his size advantage I could probably beat him in a match. Chris bellowed, "Shut up, Fred!"

Now, Chris was well over 300 pounds, and I wasn't too thrilled about the idea of locking horns with him. Fred and Spade would talk out an idea and Fred would end by saying something like "And then Jay can come out and pin Chris." Chris was turning red and my stomach was churning. Spade got into it, too, and began goading Chris. They both told Chris that if they had to bet, their money was on me to win the wrestling match. With that, it was on.

Chris squared himself in front of me, in what was more of a football stance than a wrestling stance. I crouched into a proper wrestling stance, figuring I might as well *look* like I could take him. I kept my arms out in front of me and countercircled Chris. Spade and Fred grew tired of all the dancing and started hollering that we were both chickenshit. Farley hollered, "Shut up, David!" and turned his head. At that moment I sprung forward and made the terrible mistake of shooting in on Chris's leg. I grabbed hold of his enormous thigh and tucked my head up against his hip for a single-leg take-down. Chris simply collapsed forward, smothering me. I fell to the carpet with all of Chris on top of me.

From years of wrestling I was preprogrammed to fall

facedown and immediately tuck my arms in close to my sides. The move is called turtling, and it prevents your opponent from executing any moves. Chris wasn't interested in moves. For the next five minutes he just sat on my back bouncing up and down like a little kid. It felt like my spine was beginning to crumble like a bag of potato chips. Chris kept bouncing up and down shouting, "Ha, ha! Ha, ha! Jay! Jay! Jay!"

I was going to become a cripple in the graphics room. I tried to reason with him. I waited for him to be in the air during one of his bounces so I could inhale enough to speak. When he landed back down on top of me, I calmly whispered, "Chris, seriously, you are going to break my back." He just kept clapping his hands, bouncing up and down, and shouting my name. I tried again and again. "Chris, if you keep bouncing on me, you are going to break my back. Please stop. You win." Spade intervened and said, "Get the fuck off of him, Farley." It was like an older brother chastising a little brother. Chris got up and asked me if he won. "Yes, Chris," I said. "You won." And then what was left of me hobbled into the men's room.

I splashed some water on my face and stared at myself in the mirror. I was pissed at myself for shooting in on his legs. I was so soundly defeated and humiliated, yet I wanted a rematch. I headed back to my office, and as I passed through the writers' room, I overheard Chris telling Jim Downey how he kicked my ass. He was sitting on the same gray couch Norm was on when Ian poured water on him for smoking. There were about nine writers at the table and with them were the cohosts, Alec Baldwin and Kim Basinger.

Downey saw me first, and before Chris could see me, he said, "I bet if Jay Mohr walked in here right now he could beat you in a rematch." Chris cursed him and Downey taunted: "No, Chris, I swear to God, you must have gotten lucky. Jay was, like, a state champion wrestler!" Some of the writers had seen me by now and started chiming in. They would murmur, "Yeah, I would have to put my money on Jay," or "You got lucky, Chris." I thought, Fuck it, and walked into the room.

Downey's eyes got wide. "Well," he said, "I'll be a son of a gun! Here's Jay now." Farley gave me a dismissive wave with his hand and the challenge was on. "Let's go again, bitch! You got lucky!" I yelled.

Chris reached out and grabbed my arm. I rushed toward him, and because he was in the act of standing up as he grabbed me, I caught him off balance. He was now standing up to the side of the couch and starting to fall down before I made contact. When he grabbed my arm, he had pulled me downward. Now that he was on his way to the ground I was in a perfect position to do something. I wrapped my left arm around his left leg behind the knee, keeping my right arm free so I could wait and see how he landed before I decided how to use it.

When Chris hit the carpet, he sort of curled up a little and rolled on his side. His chin was a few inches from his chest, so I took my right arm, shot it around his neck, and grabbed my other hand. As soon as I hit the ground, I stuck my right knee in his ribs, forming the perfect cradle. I placed my forehead against his temple and pushed into it as hard as I could. I was trying to crush his skull.

I kept driving my knee into his ribs and my forehead into his temple. I clasped my hands until they went numb. I knew that if Chris escaped, he would kill me. It didn't matter what happened next. I won. The move may have happened by accident, but it looked perfect and everyone had seen it. They also saw Chris's face turn redder more from embarrassment than the knee in the ribs. Neither one of us said anything to signify the end of the rematch, but we both stopped at the same time.

I scurried to my feet and darted out of the room toward the elevators, leaving my coat and belongings behind. I thought I should get out of there as fast as humanly possible. As I left the writers' room, I could hear all the guys riding Chris. Just as I pushed the down button, I heard a rumbling in the hallway. People were laughing and cheering.

I looked up and saw Alec Baldwin, a huge grin on his face, walking with Chris and the rest of the writers. In the back of the approaching mob was Kim Basinger. Chris was walking like a mummy. His eyes were rolled back in his head and his arms were stretched out in front of him. The night elevators were in an alcove to the side of the hallway. I had nowhere to go.

Chris grabbed me behind the head and we tied up. I

reminded myself not to shoot in on his legs. Chris threw his arms around me, pushing me left and right. I kept my center of gravity low and managed to stay on my feet. The more Chris threw me from side to side, the more I could feel how strong he was. I figured that win, lose, or draw, I should probably get it over with.

I took the palm of my right hand and pushed in against the outside of his left elbow. As Chris resisted, I slid my hand under his left elbow and jammed it upward. Chris's left arm swung up in the air and I ducked my head through his armpit and back around behind him. My ass and the rest of my body squirted through the same space at the same time as my head. I was now standing behind him with my hands clasped around his belly, a wrestling move known as a duck-under. The next step of the move was to lift your opponent up and dump him on the mat. Because I couldn't lift Chris, I planned to trip him.

I squeezed him tighter to me, hoping that he thought I was going to try and lift him. He took the bait and lowered his weight and surged forward. I put my right calf around Chris's kneecap and pushed forward and down. As Chris lifted his leg to escape, he crashed to the ground, with me on his back. The walls shook and I thought I had broken both of my hands, which were trapped under his belly. I wiggled my hands loose and noticed that my right one was bleeding from scraping across Chris's belt buckle. I slapped Chris on the ass as I got up. At that exact moment, the elevator bell rang and the doors slid open.

There were five or six people in the elevator and they

were obviously coming from the Rainbow Room. The men wore tuxedos and the women had on lovely gowns. There was an NBC security guard wearing a black sports jacket standing there behind the tuxedos, the lovely gowns, the perfume, and the money. I stepped onto the elevator and frantically pushed the close door button. But the doors stayed open and Chris got up off of the blue carpet and walked toward me.

Chris had raspberries stretching across both forearms and a look on his face that scared me shitless. He was going to tear my head off and feed it to the tuxedoed Rainbow Room patrons. I had now beaten him twice. When he won the first match, it was in front of Spade and Fred Wolf, but when I beat him, it was in front of everyone—most important, Alec Baldwin and Kim Basinger.

The elevator doors weren't going to close in time, and Chris was going to kill me. I pointed at him and tapped the guy next to me. "Holy shit!" I said. "That's Chris Farley." The guy said, "That *is* Chris Farley!" and the elevator erupted.

All the drunken rich people recognized Chris and started waving to him and saying hello. Not wanting to deal with them, Chris turned and walked back through the mob. The elevator doors closed and I wondered whether it would ever be safe to go back to work. The security guard and the rich people talked the whole way down about how they couldn't believe they had seen him.

None of them asked me why I was bleeding.

SEVEN

FIGHT OR FLIGHT?

IT WAS a typical Thursday night. As usual, the show needed to be rewritten, mostly to cut time and punch up the jokes on each sketch. But what the show didn't need was fifteen grown men sitting around a table arguing over what to name a fictitious high school that would be seen in the opening of one of the sketches. So we sat around for hours. Someone would say, "Washington High School," and three other people would roll their eyes and say, "No!"

I never grasped who was steering us, but I was sure we were going nowhere fast. I began to sweat. In intervals, almost like contractions, I would feel unreasonable terror. I didn't care what they named the school, yet I found myself blurting out names like Central and Montclair just to put a stop to it. But on it went—the naming of a high school, an act with no bearing on the content of the sketch whatsoever.

Leaving the writers' room during rewrites was verboten. If you so much as got up to make a phone call or stretch your legs, Jim Downey would ask where you thought you were going. One Thursday around 3:00 A.M., Tom Davis walked out of his office through the writers' room holding a suitcase and his guitar. He was wearing a knee-length parka and a pair of bright red mittens, and he had a scarf wrapped around his neck. Two-thirds of the way on his journey through the room, Downey asked incredulously, "Tom, where do you think you're going?" Tom Davis stopped, turned toward Downey, and replied, "The bathroom." Then he walked straight to the elevators. I envied Tom's courage. About as far as I went was later in the winter when Dave Attell and I sneaked out at night to do stand-up downtown. We would act like we were going to the bathroom and return three hours later to discover that no one had even noticed we were gone.

I spent each Thursday night planning my escape. I thought constantly about how to organize my flight. Rewrites in the wintertime were murder, because winter is high school basketball season. Jim Downey was a rabid high school basketball fan. His high school alma mater in the suburbs of Chicago was a national powerhouse during the years I worked on the show. Jim would bring in tapes of the high school team's games and make us all watch them. His enthusiasm was unbridled and contagious. With Downey pointing out the highlights in the game, you wouldn't even realize that two hours had passed at first. But after a while, you began to notice.

I grew to resent Jim Downey's precious high school. I mulled over the idea of bringing in some home movies to show everyone. Sometimes as late as two in the morning, Downey would put a high school basketball game tape in his VCR, which meant you were gonna be there a while. With Harvard-educated guys arguing over the name of a high school, we had an uncanny ability to always be way behind schedule. Downey would raise his voice a little and say, "C'mon, guys, we have eleven sketches to rewrite!" to rally us. We would all focus long enough to finish one sketch—and then Downey would put another tape in the VCR.

It wasn't until my second season that I realized that Downey was going through a divorce. He lived by himself and was lonely. His whole M.O. of making us watch those high school basketball tapes and arguing over the name of a meaningless fictitious high school was so that he could have some company during the early morning hours between the time that the writers left and when the other staff came in the next morning.

At one point during the debate over the name of the high school, I had to make a quick decision: leave or kill. I couldn't leave the building because all of my belongings were in my office on the opposite end of the writers' room. There was no way to collect my things and discreetly exit. So I began doing some deep breathing at the table to catch my breath. I looked around to see who was in the room. I wanted to see who was there. I needed to know who was there. I needed to see how many people were going to watch me have a heart attack.

During my first year on *Saturday Night Live,* I worked pretty regularly doing stand-up on the college circuit. Just getting the show made me an easier sell, but even those trips were fraught with peril.

On one trip, I was sitting in Newark Airport waiting to catch a flight when I felt a surge of fear flow through my body. I looked around the terminal and saw everyone living their lives. None of them had any idea mine was about to end. It wasn't fair. I didn't want to die around these people. I tried to make eye contact so I could judge by their reaction if I looked as if I were dying. No one flinched. They all acted normal. The flight number was announced and people began boarding the plane. I looked at the tunnel that led to the plane and all the people lined up and huddled together in it as if they were in a meat grinder. It seemed preposterous to follow them. I thought of what it would be like to feel this way while climbing through 30,000 feet. Boarding the plane was the equivalent of a death sentence. I picked up my bags and walked outside to catch a cab back to my apartment.

To say the least, this made my agent's job difficult. I freaked out at the last second and ditched a few gigs in a row. The shows I managed to make it to, I was so scared of panicking while I was there that I couldn't speak to anybody.

I was late a lot, too. I had a show at Millikin University in Illinois. I flew from Newark Airport into Chicago's O'Hare for a connecting flight to somewhere else. The plane was not a puddle jumper or a prop, it was just smaller than the one before it. I stared at the shiny side of the plane and pictured the tube inside that waited to suffocate me. I wasn't getting on. I walked to the rental car counters and asked them how far it was to Millikin. They all told me it was a five-hour drive. No problem, I thought. If I rent a car and leave now, I'll be only an hour late to the show.

However, I had another problem. I wasn't old enough to rent a car. Hertz, Avis, Budget, Dollar—I begged them one by one to rent me a car. I told them that I was on *Saturday Night Live* and I was on my way to my own concert. The law is the law, they all told me. You have to be twenty-five to rent a car. I was going to have to hitchhike, steal a car, or miss another show.

I took a seat on the edge of the baggage carousel and shivered at the thought of getting on another plane just to get back home. Every asshole in the world was renting cars that day. They had no idea how great they had it. They could walk up to a desk, and if they had a driver's license saying they were twenty-five, someone would hand them the keys to a car. Assholes, all of them. They came and they left, into their rented cars and away from the planes and the tubes.

My reverie was broken when a woman at one of the counters where I had already begged called me over. She told me discreetly that she loved *Saturday Night Live* and would rent me a car but cautioned me that I couldn't tell anyone. It was a deal.

I drove for five hours and passed nothing. I was safe. Nothing else existed. If I let any sensory information in, I would start an avalanche that I couldn't possibly stop. I did the show and counted each routine after I finished it. I had been keeping a list of how many jokes I could get through before I started to panic. At Millikin University I stopped counting somewhere in the teens and eventually finished the show. I had a car outside that made me feel safer. When I finished the show, I said good night and walked out of the theater and back to my car. I pulled out of the school grounds and very quietly made my way back to Chicago.

That night I slept in a motel near O'Hare that was so disgusting I didn't crawl under the blankets. I lay on top of the bed with my clothes on and counted my heartbeats. There was a small stove next to the bed that could only have been used to cook crack. I checked the walls for clocks and faces. I thought of the tube. I would have to board a plane in the morning, sit in that tube, and walk through the meat grinder with everyone else. People in the next room were fighting, and I thought that this would be the perfect time and place to die.

But I didn't die, and I kept not dying. I woke up every single day. I went to work and wondered what fucking plan everyone else was following. They all seemed fine. They wrote, they talked, they got on the elevators, they ate, and they did it all so effortlessly. They seemed to do it one day at a time. Just like everyone else in the world at any other job. Me, I didn't know how long a day was anymore.

It was six or seven weeks into the show and everyone seemed to have fallen into some sort of a pattern. I had fallen into a pattern of acting as if I were normal. I don't remember which show it was or who the guests were, but I remember the breaking point. I remember going completely mad.

I was in my dressing room watching the show's dress rehearsal on the closed circuit television that hung from the ceiling in the corner. It was the second or third week in a row that I wasn't in any sketches. I lay back in the recliner chair and positioned myself directly under the television so that if it fell out of the ceiling, it would knock me out. I just lay there and watched sketch after sketch that I wasn't in. What happened next, I later learned, was my fight-or-flight mechanism kicking in.

At the time, I would have called it going crazier than a shithouse rat. I had experienced panic before this particular night, but this one was special—special in a bad way. I jumped from the recliner and ran to the elevators and into the streets and into the night.

I ran all the way back to my apartment—forty-two blocks away.

When I reached my apartment, my roommate was sitting on the couch reading a book and not dying. I told him I had to go to the emergency room for a heart attack. He raised an eyebrow at me, since I had told him this several times before. He refused to take me to the hospital, so I decided to run there.

When I hit the street again, I began thinking of how at a hospital they would put me on a stretcher and the claustrophobia from that would kill me slower than a heart attack. I decided to take a bath to relax, so I doubled back to my apartment. As the tub filled, I looked in the medicine cabinet for some aspirin. There, on one of the shelves, stood the most beautiful of all pill bottles. It gleamed and glistened and glowed. It was filled with Valium. I had never taken Valium before that night, but I had convinced a doctor to give me a prescription to help me with my flying situation. I swallowed one beautiful blue pill and climbed into a bath that was unfortunately not deep enough to drown in.

About half an hour later the Valium began to kick in. I didn't feel better, I felt euphoric. I wasn't dying. For the first time in a month and a half, I didn't have a hot spinning asterisk inside of me. My insides were fine with being on the inside. I climbed out of the tub, wrapped myself in a towel, and phoned my parents. I told them I had almost died at work, but I had taken a Valium and now felt better. They told me that is exactly what happens when you take Valium, and asked if I had any idea what time it was.

I did indeed: It was time to go back to work. I didn't go back that night out of any sense of duty or responsibility. I went back simply to see what it was like to be inside the walls of the building while not dying. I decided to take a taxi back to Midtown. I sat in the back of the cab and struck up a conversation with the driver. He didn't speak much English, but it didn't matter. I was speaking; someone was responding. We passed street signs. I looked out the window at all the bars and restaurants, with patrons spilling out onto the sidewalk. For the first time I could remember I was just like them . . . living.

When I arrived at 30 Rock, I tipped the driver twenty bucks. I rode the night elevators up to the eighth floor and said hello to everyone I saw. The elevator was regular-sized and the walls were just as wide when I got off as when I got on. Since the first day I had arrived at the show, I had kept my panic and fear to myself. From the time the Valium kicked in, I felt an urge to tell anyone who would listen how great I felt. When I walked into the studio, the show was nearly half over. Since I wasn't in anything, I roamed around saying hello to anyone. I was smiling.

I dropped in on Sarah Silverman, whose dressing room was next to mine. She wasn't in any sketches either that week. We sat and talked for a few seconds before I told her about how I had almost died and ran home and took a Valium and now felt better. Sarah's eyes lit up and she said, "You had a panic attack. You have *got* to see my doctor! She's the best!"

How the hell did Sarah Silverman know I had a panic attack? What was a panic attack? More important, how did I get in touch with her doctor? Sarah wrote a number down on the back of one of the pages of a sketch that neither of us were in. "You have to call her," she said, handing me the number. "She saved my life."

I walked from Sarah's dressing room to mine and dialed the number. Since it was past midnight on a Saturday, the answering machine picked up. The outgoing message said that if it was an emergency, I could page the doctor and she would get back to me as soon as possible. Figuring that living your life in a constant fear of dying was an appropriate emergency, I paged her.

To my surprise, by the time I got home from the wrap party, there was a message on my answering machine from the doctor herself. In the message, she stated matter-of-factly that it sounded like I was suffering from a basic panic disorder and she could see me first thing Monday morning. All I had to do was survive Sunday.

I woke up Sunday feeling like a zombie from the combination of red wine and Valium from the night before. I stayed in bed all day and counted my breaths until Monday rolled around. At 8:30 A.M., I showered, shaved, and went to visit the woman who would save my life.

The doctor had an office in a hospital on Second Avenue. To reach the elevators to her office, you had to walk through the emergency room. I found this incredibly comforting. If anything went wrong or if I flipped out, treatment was at hand. I sat in a small waiting room and wondered what was wrong with everyone I saw coming and going. Were they experiencing panic attacks, too? Eventually an attractive young woman walked out of a door and introduced herself.

"Hello," she said, shaking my hand. "Come in."

I looked around her office and was a little disappointed that there wasn't a couch. I had always seen people on television and in the movies lie on a couch and spill their guts to a shrink, who would scribble notes down on a legal pad. In this doctor's office, I had to settle for a chair across from her desk. It didn't matter. I was there and was going to tell her everything.

I spoke for about twenty minutes straight. When I was done, she told me I did indeed have a panic disorder, which was most common for men in my age group who are actors and medical interns. Basically, it affects people who come from structure and are thrown into structure-less environments. She asked me if panic ran in my family. I had never given it much thought, but on the spot I remembered that both my father and one of my sisters had had episodes during my childhood.

Before I finished saying the word *sister,* the doctor had written out a prescription for something called Klonopin. She told me I was lucky to have seen her so soon. Many people, she explained, go for years experiencing panic attacks before seeking help. What struck me during this first meeting with the doctor was that she seemed rather nonplussed about the entire thing. I was going on and on about my claustrophobia—how I couldn't eat out, couldn't fly, couldn't go to ball games or take elevators or subways or even be the passenger in a car. Her attitude was, Yeah, yeah, I get it. Panic. Here's your prescription. Let's see how it works on you.

One thing was clear: She certainly wasn't as alarmed as I was. She acted as if I had told her I had a sore throat and she was giving me lozenges. She told me she was starting me out on a low dosage of one milligram a day of Klonopin, and that we would meet back in her office in a few days to see how everything worked out. She shook my hand good-bye and I walked out of her office into the elevators and then through the emergency room with my future written on a piece of paper with her signature on it.

I walked home and stopped at a pharmacy on 14th

Street to fill my prescription. The old man behind the counter told me it would take thirty minutes. He asked me if I wanted to come back later. I laughed out loud and told him I would wait for it.

I sat in the pharmacy for the next half hour at one of those do-it-yourself blood pressure stations. I monitored my blood pressure continuously for thirty minutes. Each time the air inflated around my arm, I was sure it would get stuck and I would have to rip the entire machine out of the ground to escape.

When my pills were ready, the pharmacist called my name, and I took my pill bottle of Klonopin and opened it before he could put it in a bag. I ingested my first Klonopin pill while standing at the counter, thinking that this is probably how drug addicts behave. I walked home to St. Mark's Place with a half-milligram tablet of Klonopin in my stomach and a pill bottle with fifty-nine more in my pocket.

By the time I reached my apartment, I felt sandbagged and groggy. The feeling of heaviness gave way to a primal exhaustion that barely allowed me to take off my clothes. I lay down to take a nap and slept for three hours without moving.

When I awoke, I lay absolutely still, a practice I had fallen into so I could time how long it took for the storm clouds I would carry around with me for the rest of the day to roll into my chest. I waited for an hour and realized that the storm wasn't coming. I wasn't made out of eggshells. I was human. I looked at my hands, my arms, my feet, my skin to see if any of it bothered me. I took my pulse over and over, and it was always around sixty—the same as any other human being who has just woken up. It was as if someone told me that the ice was thick enough to walk on, so I stepped out of my bed with a renewed confidence that I wasn't going to fall through and drown in the cold water.

I felt normal, which for me was nothing short of euphoric.

It was Monday, and in a few hours I would have to go up to Lorne's office and pitch ideas to whichever host sat in the leather chair next to Jim Downey. I had no ideas and knew it didn't matter. Weeks ago I would've been up pacing my apartment racking my brain for ideas for the looming pitch meeting. I now knew better. The pitch meeting wouldn't start until after nightfall. I didn't care about the pitch meeting; all I cared about was that I had felt normal all night long.

I cautiously made my way to the shower. I stood there and let the hot water run down my back, noting that soap was soap, towels were towels, doors were doors, and they weren't making me nervous. As I dried myself I looked in the mirror and noticed that I was ghastly thin. "Good," I thought, " 'cause I'm starving."

I got dressed and walked across the street to St. Mark's Café and ordered a 5:00 P.M. breakfast. I looked around the restaurant and wanted to hug everyone in it. I paid the bill and boarded the N/R subway to go to the office for the pitch meeting. It wasn't until I got off at 49th Street that I realized I merely felt like I had ridden the subway, nothing more, nothing less. Coming out of the stairwell from the subway, I was almost blinded by the sun, and I wondered how long it had been there.

It was 6:30 P.M. when I arrived at the seventeenth floor. When I stepped off the elevator, Mike Shoemaker was passing by, mumbling over his shoulder that the pitch meeting was about to start. I put my backpack down on the couch in my office and made my way to Lorne's office. His door was still closed, so I sat on the hallway floor and waited. I wanted to be one of the first ones there so I could sit on the big couch across from him. If I were going to be fired for having no ideas, I was going to be sitting down when the ax fell.

I have no memory of who the host or the musical guest was that week. I'd had such a life-altering experience that day that the show suddenly seemed laughably small. Lorne's door opened and people began shuffling in. I sat on the couch and looked into the faces of everyone else in the room. They all looked beaten. Defeated.

As the pitches worked their way clockwise around Lorne's desk, I heard David Spade say the words that would henceforth cut my weekly anxiety in half. When Lorne asked David for a pitch, he said, "I'm gonna work with Fred on his idea." I was startled by the revelation.

Bullshit! I thought. He doesn't have any ideas this

week either! Fred and David were buddies, so this was simply a safety net Spade grabbed to save his ass. "I'm gonna help Fred with his idea." Fred didn't seem to mind his position as the guy being gravy-trained at all.

I thought back to all the pitch meetings and all the times I had heard that sentence. How could I have been so deaf? When it was my turn to pitch, I looked around the room for someone with actual ideas who had already pitched them who I was friendly enough with to pull the sentence on. Attell!

Lorne looked at me and said, "Jay?" All eyes were on me, and because I was sitting on the couch almost everyone else was standing, looking down at me.

"I have a few things I haven't fleshed out yet, but I'm working with Attell on his idea," I said confidently. No one called bullshit on me and Attell just nodded his head. He could have blurted out, "No you're not!" But he didn't. He just nodded his head and saved me from being fired. Bless his heart.

Even though I was now medicated, everything I said seemed to make things worse. My entire life I have talked too much. If there was one thing I could change about myself, it would be my inability to close my mouth. My manager, Barry, would constantly tell me, "If you don't say anything, you can't say the wrong thing." He was right, of course, and I always knew he was right, but I continued to speak without thinking first. It's what got me into trouble as a kid, and it was now what was getting me into trouble as an adult. Most people have a filter somewhere between their brains and their mouths. Not me.

My penchant for putting my foot in my mouth began at the wrap party after my first show. I spotted Nirvana's Dave Grohl in the hallway and headed toward him. I asked him if he wanted to go smoke a joint. He looked at me like I had three heads and said to me, "I'm kind of doing the family thing right now." As he spoke, I noticed he had his arms around what looked like his mother and his grandmother.

But I really stepped in a pile of doggie doo-doo when Alec Baldwin and Kim Basinger cohosted. I was feeling trapped in another Thursday of rewrites, listening to sketch after sketch grind to a halt in front of twenty or so writers who apparently had nothing else to do with their lives.

That night, rewrites got off to an early start—meaning that the sun was still up. Someone had written a sketch about the game show *Family Feud*. In the sketch, the Baldwins were one family, and Kevin Nealon, Julia Sweeney, Sarah Silverman, and I were the other. (Alec's brothers Stephen and Billy had both agreed to be in the sketch.) That left one open spot at the end of the dais to be occupied by Tim Meadows, who would play the author James Baldwin.

As the "Family Feud" sketch was executed line by

line, I noticed that every time Kim Basinger spoke in the sketch, she had only one syllable at a time. Alec, Billy, James (Tim), and Stephen spoke in complete sentences, but when it was Kim's turn to speak, she was relegated to saying things like yes and no. The longest line she had in the sketch was "I don't know," which she was scripted to say twice. I wasn't the only one who noticed this. Sarah Silverman broke up the infighting by asking, "How come all of Kim's lines are only one word?"

Before anyone could answer I blurted out, "Because she's dumb!"

I had gotten used to no one reacting to anything I said anymore. But this time they all reacted. A hush fell over the room as everyone stopped talking. I lifted my head and looked around the table. No one would make eye contact with me. Everyone was reacting as if she was in the room when I said it—and she was. During the rewrite, Alec and Kim had made their way into the room, and they were sitting on the same couch I was on when Farley fake-puked in my lap on my first day at work. The couch was directly across from me, and Alec Baldwin and Kim Basinger were staring straight at me.

Alec Baldwin is a bear of a man, and I wondered how long it would take him to walk over to the table and cave in my skull with his fists. I realized it was time to do some quick thinking. I looked at the rest of the writers and practically cried out: "You guys have made her look dumb! We can do better than this! We have to do better than this. She's our guest, for Christ's sake!"

JAY MOHR

Alec didn't cave in my skull with his fists and Ms. Basinger was given several more lines in the sketch. Yikes. Not realizing that my attempts to save the sketch were merely to keep Alec from kicking my ass, Kim and Alec gravitated toward me that week. Considering my solitary state, I may have mistaken the fact that they sporadically spoke to me as some sort of bond I hadn't experienced with any other hosts or my coworkers. I would be walking back from the restroom and pass Alec in the hallway and he would throw a fake punch at me and say something like "How's it going?"

This was the friendliest anyone had been to me in weeks, and it was coming from a guy whose wife I had insulted. Man, I soaked it up.

EIGHT

THE MOTIVATIONAL SPEAKER

CHRIS FARLEY was the most beautiful person I have ever met. You wanted him around all the time. You craved his presence. You wanted to hear his stories. You wanted him to answer the phone when it rang in your office. The man was just one giant beating heart, and that heart was full of kindness. He was a genuine, loving creature, one battling horrible demons.

Chris compared his problem to four cylinders: drugs, alcohol, food, and depression. He told me that each time he pushed one cylinder down, another rose. If he managed to push three down simultaneously, the fourth would skyrocket. The entire time I worked at *SNL*, I never saw Chris on drugs or intoxicated, or for that matter even drinking an alcoholic beverage. I, however, was an alcoholic. You know who is and who isn't. You know when someone with a disease has been up all night partying. If you are that type of partier, there's no moderation. It's drinking from sunset to sunrise and doing a couple of eightballs along the way.

His weight soared in the two years I was on the show. That was the cylinder that was skyrocketing—his eating. He would also have three huge cups of black coffee before read-through, like a guy doing shots at a bar. Despite his weight, there were times when he looked absolutely handsome. He'd have his hair slicked back, with the mousse making it kick out on the side, and he'd be wearing sunglasses. He would try to dress up, but at heart he was still Chicago's Second City, so he would wear the army boots with the suit.

As far as I'm concerned, Chris was also the funniest man who ever lived. No one can ever touch Farley. In basketball, there's Michael Jordan and there's everyone else. Well, there was Farley and then there was everyone else. But Farley was better than Jordan in his prime. A ball can go through the hoop only one way. More than anyone I have ever seen in the history of *Saturday Night Live,* Chris made each segment he was a part of absolute madness. He fed off the live audience, and they couldn't get enough of him.

I've never seen a performer showered with love as Farley was in the "Little Women" figure-skating sketch when David Hyde Pierce hosted. The characters (played by Pierce, Farley, Spade, and Janeane Garofalo) were all dressed in costumes from the 1800s. As they took turns on the ice rink, doing figure eights and showing off, Farley criticized them with foppy lines like "I think you should pay more attention to your schoolwork." At the end, as everyone argued with everyone else, Farley went out to skate and broke the ice. When Farley fell through the trapdoor into the ice-cold water, he screamed, "Shut the hell up, you stupid whores, and get me out of here!" As the little women came to his aid, he pulled them all in the water with him.

At the end of the sketch, everyone climbed out of the water quickly to escape the cold—except Farley. He didn't pull himself out until the show had gone to commercial and the band began to play. When he emerged from the hole, his coat had fallen off and he was clutching the soggy garment in his hands. He was standing directly under the cantilevered balcony seats and in front of the people seated on the floor in front of the stage where the sketch had been performed. Dripping wet, Farley held his clothes over his head like a cross between an ancient gladiator and David Lee Roth. He was an absolute god and a sopping wet mess, and the crowd went berserk.

What was true for the audience was true for the performers: If you were in a sketch with Farley, you were going to have some serious fun. You never knew what craziness Chris was going to pull out of his bag of tricks.

Even though the sketch's lines and all the parts were written on cue cards, Chris always managed to come up with something fresh and new. He also had the uncanny ability to make everyone else in the sketch tremble while holding in his own laughter. It was as if Chris was on a mission; if he didn't make you laugh, he had somehow failed.

Martin Lawrence was hosting the show near the end of my first season, and a "Motivational Speaker" sketch had been written starring him and Chris. The premise was based on the *Scared Straight!* program. I was only about eleven years old when I first saw *Scared Straight!* It was the first time I had ever heard swearing on television. Wayward kids were assembled inside a jail in front of a group of prisoners. Each kid thought he was pretty hot stuff, and because they were chosen for the *Scared Straight!* program, you could bet they were capital *B* bad. The prisoners would take turns screaming in the kids' faces about busting open their assholes and breaking the little motherfuckers down. I couldn't believe my luck. I was watching network television unsupervised and being treated to a feast of vulgarity. Now, ten years later, I found that the mere premise of parodying *Scared Straight!* made me laugh out loud. Better yet, I was also going to be in the sketch.

In fact the entire cast was in the sketch. Phil Hartman played the warden who told Meadows, Spade, Sandler, Schneider, and me that he was going to introduce us to his hardest inmates. First Martin came onstage wearing a cornrow wig and flashing an enormous gold tooth. Martin delivered the speech and then told us he was going to bring out the baddest homeboy he knew, a man named Matt Foley who was in jail for failure to pay child support (Farley).

In dress rehearsal, Chris played it pretty close to the script. He never touched Martin Lawrence's wig and he stuck to the cue cards. I wondered to myself what adjustments he would make between dress rehearsal and airtime to make us all laugh. At the end of the sketch, Chris was supposed to dance around to make a point and accidentally crash through the wall of the jail. After Chris made the hole in the wall, all of us were to get up from our seats and escape through the hole. Then Chris would reenter and deliver his final line.

But Sandler came up with an idea to give Chris a taste of his own medicine. For all the times Chris made us laugh during a sketch, we would get him back at the end of this one. Instead of all of us running out through the hole in the wall, Sandler decided that we should all fall down on top of Chris so he wouldn't be able to get back up to reenter and say his final line. Though everyone signed off on the plan, I secretly wondered if we would actually go through with it.

The dress rehearsal of the sketch went off as scripted.

There was a large gymnastics mat on the other side of the wall for Chris to fall on. We all sat on the mat after escaping from the jail and peeked back through the hole at Chris delivering his line. We laughed offstage, knowing that what Chris was saying wouldn't be said again on the live show.

Martin Lawrence provided enough of a distraction so that no one was focusing on what high jinks Farley might toss in. Knowing that the dress rehearsal wasn't being aired on TV, Martin delivered an X-rated monologue. It lasted four minutes long, and most of it was about going down on a woman who tastes nasty. When he finished, we all waited for Lorne to say something to Martin about making sure he toned down the monologue for the live show. Lorne droned on and on to every conceivable technical employee. People whom I never noticed worked on the show were getting notes about the sound being too high or the lights being a bit low. Camera angles were dissected and re-dissected. At one point, the wardrobe people were asked to make sure the costume changes were timely. After thirty minutes, Lorne told us all to have a great show. As we got up to leave and prepare for the show, Lorne looked across his office at Martin and said, "Martin? Are we okay?" Martin nodded his head and that was that. I couldn't decide if Lorne was afraid to confront Martin, or if Lorne was being classy by not confronting Martin with the cast in the room.

The live show started and Don Pardo shouted, "Ladies and gentlemen . . . Martin Lawrence!" We all held our breath. Some of the cast had gathered in the studio to watch Martin and listen to what was going to come out of his mouth. That was the beauty of live television: Whatever was said was said, and there were no second takes.

Amazingly, Martin's opening monologue was very similar to the one in the dress rehearsal. He talked about women being funky down there and suggested that they might want to insert a Tic Tac in their ass. He never actually swore, but the content of the monologue all but ensured that the show would never be reaired or shown as a repeat. Considering it was a show I was actually a part of, I found that slightly upsetting. But the upside to knowing the show was now a lame duck was that the repercussions wouldn't be as harsh for us pinning Farley to the ground and ruining a sketch.

It was a commercial break and the "Motivational Speaker" sketch was scheduled to be next. We were all changing into our hoodlum clothes that the wardrobe people made sure were properly and promptly hung in our dressing rooms. As I changed, I discovered a terrifying error. The pants I was supposed to wear in the skit didn't have any pockets, which meant that I had nowhere to put my extra tablet of Klonopin.

I had been carrying extra medication with me everywhere I went in case I started to have a panic attack. I had taken to wearing blue jeans because of the extra square Klonopin pocket above my right thigh. When I had to wear slacks or a police uniform in a sketch, I always found a place to hide my extra pill, usually in the back left pocket. I had also worked out a plan. If I started to have a panic attack on live TV, I would wait until the camera was on somebody else, slip my hand into the pocket, and quickly swallow the pill. I never anticipated that the wardrobe department would outfit me with clothes with no pockets. How could they? How hard is it to give a guy pants with pockets in them? I froze in my dressing room and looked at my blue jeans on the floor at my feet. I made an executive decision to wear the jeans in the sketch.

But just as I started to unbutton my wardrobe pants, stage manager Joe Dicso's booming voice came over the intercom. "Thirty seconds to 'Motivational Speaker.' Thirty seconds. We gotta go, we gotta go!" I wasn't going to make it. There was no way I could change out of the wardrobe pants and into my jeans and then run onto the stage in thirty seconds. I jammed my fingers into the small pocket of my jeans and fished out two Klonopin pills, and then I ran through the hallways of the eighth floor, rebuttoning my wardrobe pants and clutching two pills in what was now a very sweaty hand. I was going to have to hold the pills in my hand during the sketch. As I took my seat in the makeshift jail set, my hands were sweating so profusely that I was worried the pills would dissolve in my palms in the middle of the sketch. Logically, I could have taken the pill as a preventive measure, but there is no logic to panic, so that thought never crossed my mind. Besides, what if I needed them in the middle of the skit?

We came back from commercial and the stage lights went up. As I sat in my seat, I swiftly transferred the pills to my left hand, out of view of the camera. Phil Hartman began speaking and I hung my arm motionless at my side, trying to leave small cracks between my fingers to ventilate my palms so the pills wouldn't dissolve. I had to be careful not to make the cracks between my fingers so wide that the pills rolled out between my knuckles onto the floor.

Phil finished his bit and introduced us to Martin Lawrence with his cornrows, his gold tooth, and his prison blues. As Martin began speaking, I started to become short of breath and feel the urge to jump from my chair and walk off the set. If I walked off the set on live television, I thought to myself, I'll never have to return. I could just spend the rest of my life somewhere else wearing pants with pockets in them. It almost seemed like a fair trade-off.

My mind wandered. I remembered the doctor telling me that no one in the history of medicine had ever died of a panic attack. I remembered her telling me about desensitization exercises, and thought that they seemed pretty drastic. I also thought of how incredibly unfair it all was. Why couldn't I just be like everyone else on the show? That's all I wanted. I wanted to be able to sit in a chair during a sketch and watch Martin Lawrence explain to us how in prison young punks like us could be sold to other inmates for a pack of cigarettes.

In an attempt to refocus, I stared at Martin's gold tooth and watched his mouth form words. I wondered how long it would take me to become a lip-reader, and I wondered why I wasn't already unconscious. I was now clutching the pills firmly so I could feel them in my palm, which made me feel marginally better. I no longer cared what happened to the pills. If they were crushed or dissolved in my hand, I would simply lick the Klonopin dust from my palms in front of America.

Then Farley happened.

I didn't actually hear Martin introduce Matt Foley (Chris) into the sketch, but he must have, because the door to the cell opened and Chris exploded onto the set. He was wearing prison blues and eyeglasses, just as in dress rehearsal, but as he entered, something about his appearance was drastically different. Prior to his entrance, Chris had taken the time to make gigantic sweat stains stretching from his armpits all the way down to his waist on both sides of his body. Gigantic pit stains! That was it. We all immediately burst out laughing. The audience started laughing because we were laughing, which only made us laugh harder.

As Chris fiddled with his belt and waited for the applause to die down, the stage lights glistened off his pit stains. I wondered at what point he decided he would add the pit stains to the sketch. It didn't matter; once again, he had us all by the balls. We were helpless. Martin's character had explained to us the bartering of young punks for cigarettes, and when the applause died down, he made a grand gesture of handing the cigarette he was holding to Chris, signifying that we were now the property of Matt Foley. He had no idea how right he was.

As Chris spoke to each of us individually, he timed when the camera was off him and on us. When the camera was on me, he said all of his lines cross-eyed. When the camera was back on him, he straightened his eyes and went back to being normal, which, for him, was being the funniest man alive. As he made his way down the line of young punks, he repeatedly crossed and uncrossed his eyes. We were all laughing out loud and nothing could stop us. It was sheer comedic brilliance. Despite the fact that the cameras were over his shoulder and twenty feet away, Chris knew the exact moment that the camera switched shots. I had never laughed like that before in my life—and I had no idea I was about to laugh even harder. Farley filled the stage, leaving no room for panic. The sun was out and the shadows were gone.

Whenever Chris or Martin said a line, they would make a grand gesture of passing the cigarette back and forth, the way the boys in *Lord of the Flies* used the conch. Farley finished his first paragraph of dialogue and handed the cigarette back to Martin. Chris's line (I know this because it was written on the cue card) was supposed to be: "Sold! Five bitches to the homie in the cornrows." But what came out of his mouth instead was: "Sold! Five bitches to the cornie in the homie rows!" He then paused, looked directly into camera, and said "Oops!"

I was never so grateful or appreciative of my coworkers as I was at that moment, because thankfully, they were all laughing as hard as me. I would have stood out if I wasn't laughing. Even Phil Hartman was smirking, and I had never seen him come close to breaking character on the air.

As the sketch was nearing the end, Chris began dancing around and making his way toward the wall that he was going to fall through. He tripped over his own feet and obliterated the breakaway wall, falling onto his back on top of the gymnastics mat. The rest of us started running for the hole in the wall—and it wasn't lost on me that we were now literally escaping the madness of Farley and the powerlessness he incited in us.

But instead of going through the wall one by one as scripted, we all raced to be the first one out of the sketch and on top of Chris. Five of us threw our bodies through the hole, and as we landed on Chris's chest, we began screaming and squealing like children. We finally had him where we wanted him. There was now close to a thousand pounds of laughing idiots on top of Chris Farley on the gym mat.

No more than one second passed before Chris realized what we were doing. Chris didn't panic, get angry, or even laugh. He simply picked us off of his body one by one like we were leaves. When we dove back on top of him, he removed us two by two. He then started throwing us aside like trash bags so he could be back onstage in time to deliver his line. With time to spare, he was on his mark, finishing the sketch, while we lay on the gym mat rubbing our bumps and bruises and gasping for air. We peeked through the hole in the wall just as we had done in dress rehearsal—except this time it was with a sense of awe at what we had just witnessed.

To this day, I don't know what happened to those pills.

In my second season, Farley struck again in a "Motivational Speaker" sketch. I was only in the sketch because Spade had been trying to score at a party full of models. He thought his chances were good, so he had called Downey and asked to be removed from the sketch. He then wouldn't have to return for rehearsals that night. After Downey told me about Spade, it became a running joke between us. Whenever David would call and say he wasn't making rehearsal, Downey would hang up and give me Spade's part in the sketch. The more famous Spade became, the better his odds to score a model became, and the more sketches I got in.

In this "Motivational Speaker" sketch, Michael Mc-Kean was playing a wealthy Spanish father of two. He explained to his kids, who were played by Morwenna Banks and me, that he had called the United States to enroll the help of a motivational speaker (that is to say, Farley as Matt Foley). Chris's part was written entirely in Spanish. America had probably seen Matt Foley ten times—but never speaking Spanish.

Farley entered the stage, shouting at the top of his lungs: "Hola, mis niños! Me llama señor Matt Foley!" Keeping a straight face was impossible. The audience erupted when Chris delivered the money line for the first time in Spanish: "Van cerca del río!"

McKean's character explained to Señor Foley that both he and his children spoke excellent English, so speaking in Spanish was not necessary. Chris as Matt Foley responded, "Padre, donde por favor and ferme ton grande YAPPER!" That's when I was supposed to say my line. It was simple. All I had to do was open my mouth and say, "Señor Foley, where did you learn your Spanish? Taco Bell?"

The problem was that Chris had screamed his line so loud into McKean's ear that he covered him in spittle, causing him to move back a step. I struggled to keep from becoming a member of the audience myself. Although I was in the sketch, I was being treated to an incredible performance. I bit my tongue and tried to think of things that weren't funny. I thought of dead babies and naked grandmothers, but resistance was futile. Chris was standing on the stage, but he was also taking up all of the space between my ears. Finally I decided that if I was a teenager and Matt Foley was in my living room in Spain, screaming into my father's ear in terrible Spanish, I would think it was funny and most likely giggle. I said the line and laughed at the same time, making it barely audible.

Then Chris sauntered across the set toward me and put his hand on top of my head and began to tussle my hair. To the audience it looked endearing—but we all knew better. As he shouted, "Muy cómico es el Paul Rodriguez?" he continued to rub his hand back and forth until my black wig was now draped over one of my ears.

For the rest of the sketch I was delusional. I didn't know whether to fix my wig or just to continue with the wig hanging on the side of my face. The audience watched the entire process unfold, and an entirely different dimension of laughter filled the studio. Chris had all of us by the jugular. I should have been at least a little prepared. In dress rehearsal, Chris had tugged gently on the hair on my wig, making it come loose but not off. I giggled through that exchange as well. In the meeting in Lorne's office between the dress rehearsal and the live show, Lorne looked at me and said, "Jay, do you think you could do us all a favor and not laugh through the entire sketch?" I said of course, but I knew that was a lie.

The corollary to the Farley wig trick was that if people in the sketch weren't wearing wigs but Chris was, he would shake his head violently to make his own wig fall off—though not in dress rehearsal. He played it straight in dress rehearsal so he could surprise you on live television.

Farley couldn't cure writer's block, but he sure could break up the monotony. When you were stuck, he was the guy who could push you over the edge.

Late one wintry night, I was going crazy. Dave Attell and I were on a downward spiral, and we had given up. Uncle! We couldn't put anything on paper. Our writing collaboration was like waiting for a bus with a guy you know but don't talk to. We very rarely bounced ideas off each other. It was just one guy on one side of the room smoking and doodling and the other guy on the other side checking his messages and leafing through car magazines. The only spark of hope that night was this Otis Redding boxed CD set that Lorne had given all the writers for Christmas. The cover art for the CD was an early head shot of Otis, my man. Dave had poked a hole where Otis's mouth was and put a cigarette in it. On that dull, unproductive night it was the funniest thing either one of us had ever seen. We were keeled over holding our sides laughing. We needed help, so we called Chris into the office to hang out.

I'm not sure which one of us heard Chris Farley first, but it didn't matter. The moment he walked through the doorway we began laughing like little kids. You couldn't help it. He was a wrecking ball of joy.

One of us told Chris we would pay him a hundred bucks to take a dump out of our window. Farley was no dummy; he wanted our money on the table first. We were laughing so hard it took us a while to dig through our pockets and cobble together the hundred. When we did, we pooled the cash on my desk, which was next to the window. Chris stuffed the money into his pocket and opened the wide window with a wave of his arm.

Methodically, he prepared to execute. He unbuckled his pants and climbed onto my desk and then out onto the windowsill. The heels of his boots were on the outside of the window frame and his ass was dangling in the cold December air. Still fiddling with his belt buckle, Chris rested the back of his neck on the bottom of the window and balanced the rest of his enormous self outside the building to ensure that the shit fell out and not in. Seventeen floors above the dullest night in the history of man, Chris's face turned beet red as he tried desperately to squeeze a shit out the window.

Dave and I were delirious. We laughed until we saw stars, knowing that one false move and Chris would fall to his death. A snot bubble came out of Chris's nose as he pushed. Soon a tiny marble of crap dropped onto the windowsill. Chris looked up at us proudly, cracking a smile, the snot bubble still clinging to his right nostril. He craned his neck, searching around the office for something to wipe his ass with. There was a porno magazine on Attell's desk, but it was too far away to be practical. So

Chris wiped his ass with his hand. I had never seen anyone do that before.

Then Chris jumped off the window ledge and began chasing Dave and me across the office, his shit-stained paw outstretched.

We tore out of the office screaming and raced down the hallway as if we were being chased by a monster. In a way we were. We didn't stand a chance of escaping. We had laughed so hard for so long that we could hardly breathe, let alone run. I was hunched over, choking, gagging, laughing, and running for my life.

In our path was a bookshelf that jutted out from the wall, creating a single-file lane. Dave and I were shoulder to shoulder and neither of us had any plans of slowing down to be smeared with Farley's shit. Unfortunately, I was running on the bookshelf side of the hall, so if I wanted to be the first one past it, I was going to have to make a move, and soon. I concentrated on not laughing and tried to accelerate past Dave and past the bookshelf. I wasn't going to make it. I was running so hard that when my right shoulder hit the bookshelf, it spun me around and I landed flat on my back.

I had the wind knocked out of me and it felt like my shoulder was shattered, but there was no time for pain. Chris was hovering over me, waving his dark-stained hand dangerously close to my face. Now *he* was laughing hysterically. I had to think fast. There was no escape. He had me. I lay there helpless between Chris's legs, under his belly, about to eat shit.

"Farley, you fucking asshole! My arm is broken!" I screamed.

I really sold it. Chris immediately stopped laughing and a concerned look came across his face, like a child who didn't know how to help an adult. With pure innocence, he stepped back, looked down at his wounded colleague, and asked if I was okay. I rolled over onto my good shoulder, pushed myself up, and began running before my feet hit the carpet. I ran all the way to the elevators and hit the down button; I was going to go outside and throw myself in front of a cab.

As I ducked into the elevator, I looked back down the hallway and saw Chris standing motionless, a confused look on his face. To this day, thinking about that look makes me sad.

NINE

MUSIC FOR THE SOUL

HOW MANY people get to go to work and meet Kurt Cobain? I did, and for me, it was a true highlight at *Saturday Night Live*.

Nirvana was the musical guest for the first show of the year. To put it mildly, everyone was pretty excited. The album *In Utero* had just been released and the band was going to play two songs from it, "Heart-Shaped Box" and "Rape Me." "Heart-Shaped Box" was an obvious choice because it was Nirvana's first single to break from the album, but the selection of "Rape Me" had a few of us scratching our heads. I personally wondered how a show with a full-time censor would allow a song with "Rape Me" as the chorus to see the airwaves. "Rape Me" is about Kurt Cobain's feelings of being double-crossed by the media. Try explaining that to the Smith family watching the show in Utah.

We were in the middle of a writers' meeting when I heard that Nirvana was going to rehearse. I walked out of the writers' room and headed to the elevators. I didn't care if they fired me on the spot; I was watching Nirvana. This proved to be more difficult than it should have been, though I was used to walking through mazes.

In the evening only one of the main elevators was active. If you wanted to go to a different floor at night in the main elevators, you were forced to call security and secure approval from either someone on that floor or the security guard. There were a pair of night elevators toward the rear of the building. When you showed up for the job, they gave you a card for the night elevators. If you lost the card, a guard was required to walk you to and from the elevators every night.

The night elevators were primarily express elevators that shot up to the Rainbow Room. None of the floor buttons worked unless you had a card to activate them. Once you stepped off the elevator, the panel of buttons would die again. If you got on the elevator and weren't quick enough with your card, you were going to the Rainbow Room, which was not the place you want to be dumped off wearing shorts and a T-shirt. The night elevators were used the most by us and the drunken idiots in the Rainbow Room. There was a mail chute in the wall opposite the night elevators that ran through the entire building; I know this because one night I actually got off on every floor and checked. Somehow the mail chute and the elevators were connected. Whenever a night elevator would pass your floor, a long whoosh would roll out of the mail slot. In the wee hours of the morning, this was quite an eerie sound. When the offices emptied out a little bit and I was tired, miserable, and depressed, the sound of the elevator that came out of the mail slot made the entire building feel haunted.

I inserted my night elevator card in the slot and waited. Three long whooshes later, the elevator arrived. I rode alone, which seemed unfair. If a guy was about to go watch Nirvana perform, he should be able to tell someone about it. I stopped on the eighth floor and walked toward studio 8-H. I was about a hundred yards from the studio, and I could feel bass guitar in the floor and on the walls. They were tuning up!

As I approached the studio doors, I thought, What if they don't let me in? That feeling of uneasiness gave way to feelings of entitlement when I double-checked all my studio and NBC IDs. I walked into the studio, and thirty feet from me stood Kurt Cobain, Dave Grohl, and Krist Novoselic. Only twenty other people were in the entire studio. Half of those were working cameras, measuring sound, and doing lighting. The rest of us were about to enjoy a private Nirvana show.

The band looked pretty bored. As the cameras and lighting people in the control room made adjustments, the band picked at their instruments. It was obvious by their demeanor that they had done this before. If they were being told to hurry up and wait, it wasn't bothering them. Hey, whatever, never mind, right?

Kurt was wearing blue jeans and a T-shirt with a pajama top over it. It was the same pajama top I had often seen in magazine photographs. He was tiny, but he filled the entire room. Krist Novoselic, on the other hand, was gigantic. He stood six foot five, and with Kurt next to him, he looked about seven three.

As they fiddled with their instruments, each band member chirped two-word instructions to some invisible person somewhere. They were on three completely different wavelengths. It looked as if they were the technicians brought in to tune the instruments and do a sound check before the real band arrived. But they weren't. They were the biggest rock stars in the world at the time, and they were thirty feet away from me. The only thing separating me from Kurt was empty floor and his guitar. All ten of us watching could have moved forward, but we didn't. No one wanted to spook the thoroughbreds by standing too close to the stage. There were a few seconds of calm where everything in the room stopped. No fiddling, no small talk, nothing. Just a sense of calm. Then the storm hit.

The first sounds that came after the stillness were of Kurt Cobain singing "Rape Me." The song starts with the sound of a guitar and Kurt repeating the lyric a couple of times. On this take, Kurt sang the first "Rape Me" a cappella and then began strumming. It was a strong move that implied: This is the song we are playing, and if you have any problems with its content, shove it up your ass. When Kurt reached the chorus of "Rape Me," he screamed like he was dying. Until that moment, I had never heard that sound anywhere in nature. I had certainly not heard it come from a human. The sound that those three men created was mind-blowing. The hairs on my neck stood up, and I told myself that I had the greatest job on the planet.

I had never seen a band rehearse before, so I figured they took everything at half speed. Work out the kinks and save the voice. Not Nirvana. They were gone. Watching them rehearse, I saw that they knew how to do this thing only one way. There wasn't a sliver of restraint. They were merciless. Grohl beat his drums as if they owed him money. Kurt stayed pretty still, which made the sheer volume of his voice that much more impressive. Krist danced around a bit with his bass hung just over his knee, forcing him to hunch over to play it. In a word, they were ferocious.

When the song ended, the three of them just stood there as if someone had pushed stop. They looked at each other a couple of times and launched right into "Heart-Shaped Box." Again, Dave thrashed. Krist pounded. And Kurt screamed like a beautiful, wounded animal. Ferocious.

After finishing "Heart-Shaped Box," the band walked offstage. I was standing between them and their dressing room, so they had to walk past me. They did so in order of height: first Krist, to whom I said, "Great job," which drew a response of "Thanks"; then Dave, who gave me a nod; and finally Kurt, who was walking a little slower than the other guys. When Kurt was alongside me I could hardly contain myself. "That was fantastic, man," I said.

Kurt stopped walking and looked at me for a moment. After a while I extended my hand and said, "I'm Jay. I work on the show."

Kurt shook my hand and asked me what I did on the show. I told him I was a featured performer. "Do you do comedy?" he asked.

I explained to him that I did, but my primary job was to write for the cast and then try to work myself into some sketches. Sometimes, I continued, other people wrote parts for me in their sketches. Cobain nodded. "Wow," he said, "so it's kind of like being a songwriter."

"Yeah, exactly," I replied. He wished me luck and shook my hand again. He hesitated for a beat before he left. He looked like he would have traded places with me if he could have.

During my two years on *SNL*, the show had the greatest musical guests in its history. No one will ever convince me otherwise. My first year alone, we had Nirvana,

Smashing Pumpkins, Aretha Franklin, the Pretenders, Pearl Jam, Dwight Yoakam, Aerosmith, Billy Joel, Stone Temple Pilots, and James Taylor, who looked strangely like my dad. My second year, we added Eric Clapton, R.E.M., Bon Jovi, Dave Matthews Band, Hole, and Bonnie Raitt, who was the first fifty-year-old woman I have ever wanted to have sex with. There was seldom a dull moment. Green Day brought along these hard-edged groupies who had duct tape around their boots and smoked unfiltered Camels, while Nirvana's were all hot tamales. Seal was easily the strangest performer. I had read that the two scars under his eyes were the result of some tribal ritual, but it turned out they were just pink lines from some skin condition that the makeup department covered with the thick eye shadow worn by football players.

As much as I enjoyed the small, semiprivate concerts, after a while I began to feel that the lyrics of the musical guests were describing my situation on the show. They sang what I was feeling, and their lyrics also seemed to be offering me an explanation for my problems. It was almost like being in high school and having music touch your life in that indelible way it does when you are a teenager.

Looking back, it began with my first week on the show with Nirvana singing "Rape Me." Then Cypress Hill played "Insane in the Brain" the following week when my Christopher Walken "Psychic Friends Network" was unceremoniously dumped out of deference to Shannen Doherty's concern for Sean Young's feelings. The third week, Aerosmith was on the show doing "Sweet Emotion," which was the first time I appeared on camera.

Five minutes before the Aerosmith show began, Jeff Goldblum, who was hosting, gathered the cast in the greenroom. The guy was like someone from another planet. I expected the tall, nerdy guy from *The Big Chill*, but his body was ripped like an NFL wide receiver and his demeanor was smooth as silk. As everyone scurried to get ready for the show, Goldblum began smoking a fake joint. He took a long toke and then passed it to me. I passed it to Farley. As the fake joint made its way around the room two, three, then four times, nobody said a word. Before Goldblum lit the fake joint, the place was buzzing. People were struggling to pull on their bald caps. My heart was thumping with anticipation. But now the room was completely mellow.

During the show, as I stood offstage in Walken makeup watching Aerosmith perform "Sweet Emotion," I thought of my parents. They weren't able to make the show on which "Psychic Friends Network" was originally scheduled to air, but they were in the house on that Saturday when it did and Aerosmith rocked the place. I wondered what it must feel like to watch your son perform on *Saturday Night Live*. All the failed classes, all the detentions, all the groundings flew out the window. I would make them proud. My life was perfect. Sweet emotions were flowing.

At the show's after-party, I was sitting at a table with Mike Myers, who had helped me with my performance at rehearsal. The valuable trick he taught me was that if you are going to read the cue cards, which are directly above the camera lens, then you should read them the entire time so it appears as if you are looking directly into the lens. The mistake people make is going back and forth between reading the cue cards and looking into the lens, because viewers can see your eyes moving up and down.

As Myers and I were sitting in silence, Aerosmith frontman Steven Tyler walked past our table with his wife. All week, I had thought he looked like Joan Rivers. During the rehearsals, he would constantly primp himself. Tyler carried a mirror in the holster on the side of his painter's pants. The mirror wasn't a compact; it was about eight inches in diameter. It looked like a family heirloom, with small jewels lining the round edge. He looked in that mirror more than someone who lived in a house of mirrors. Somehow it was completely forgivable because he's Steven Tyler and he's a rock star. It was as if he were thinking, I want to make sure I look exactly right when I'm playing "Sweet Emotion." Tyler stopped at our table and tipped his hat. "An auspicious debut!" he said to me.

As Tyler walked away from us, I leaned across the table and started the first dialogue of the night between Mike and me. "What does *auspicious* mean?" I asked.

———

The Smashing Pumpkins performed a concert the night after their *SNL* appearance, and that was the official beginning of the end for me—and the height of my awareness that the bands were speaking to me. For weeks I'd been having trouble breathing, sleeping, eating, walking, and talking. At the time, I had no idea that there was anything known as a panic disorder; this was before my first visit to the doctor. I thought I was having multiple nervous breakdowns and mini–heart attacks that would end only after I dropped dead at the most inopportune time.

I went to see Smashing Pumpkins with Marci Klein, who was someone you wanted on your side. If you were on her bad side, you were finished. In her role as talent coordinator/coproducer, she functioned as the gatekeeper to Lorne. With long, dirty blond hair and piercing eyes, she was very attractive. She also had a real mean streak, and was a complicated person, perhaps owing to the fact that (I was told by several people) she was kidnapped as a child. Marci and I always got along pretty well, and we even formed a loose bond over our mutual love for Tabasco sauce. She always had a bottle on her desk and drizzled it on everything. I wouldn't be surprised if she put it in her coffee. Once my roommate ordered a bottle of a hot sauce called Slap My Ass and Call Me Sally, and I brought it into the office for Marci. "I've had that," she said excitedly, "but it's not as hot as this other one."

The concert was held at Roseland, a small, standing-

room-only club holding about 3,000 in Midtown Manhattan. Marci and I sat on a small elevated platform on the
side of the stage that had about fifty chairs for VIPs. The
VIPs had sacrificed one of the precious chairs to pile
their coats on, and it was about fifteen feet from Marci
and me. The house lights were on and everyone below us
was dying from the heat and from being packed in like
sardines. The only air in the room came from an air conditioner vent that was ten feet from our heads. Everyone
who was elevated was freezing; everyone who wasn't
was frying.

Standing shoulder to shoulder with the celebrities in
the VIP area, I was trying to act as nonchalant as possible.
Then Marci turned to me and barked out, "Jay, get me my
coat." I looked at the coat chair and thought of the work it
would take to even get near the chair, never mind the task
of pawing through a bunch of celebrities' coats to locate
Marci's. Anyway, I reasoned that if I pulled her coat from
the pile now and decided later that I wanted my coat, then
I would have to barge through everyone a second time. I
looked at her and said, "Why don't you get it?" I wasn't
snarky or hostile; I had merely reached indifference to my
entire situation at the show. As I finished my sentence, she
pointed at me and screamed, "I fucking discovered you!"

Now I *really* wasn't going to fetch her coat. All the
celebrities were staring at me. If they knew who I was,
they wanted to know who she was. If they didn't know
who I was, now they wanted to know. The concert hadn't

started yet and no one on the elevated, air-conditioned platform had anywhere to go. Marci turned to a stranger next to her, pointed at me again, and yelled, "I fucking discovered him!"

Then, in an act of God, the house lights went off and the concert started.

Someone at the concert had a joint and passed it my way. I took two drags and was immediately convinced that I had just smoked angel dust and would die at the concert, halfway to the chair with the coats on it. Below me, people were slam-dancing, creating a swirling whirlpool-like mosh pit. The mosh pit resembled how I felt inside. Bodies collided and people surged forward and backward, churning like the inside of my stomach.

I made my way over to the edge of the elevated VIP section and decided to let the crowd below swallow me up. I stepped off the ledge and landed with a jarring thud on the Roseland Ballroom wood floor. I was never able to penetrate the whirlpool of the crowd, so I remained on the outside, literally fighting with my fists and feet to get on the inside. No dice.

I soon found myself at the back of the ballroom, a good fifty yards from the swirling maniacs. There was a bar at the rear of the room, and I decided that if I was going to die, I was going down shit-faced drunk. Hoping that I would pass out and be trampled, I drank myself stupid but somehow kept my feet. By the time the show ended, I was slurring my speech and weaving through the crowd, searching for an exit. No matter which way I turned, I was swimming against the tide of people leaving. Like a human pinball, I bounced off person after person. The last of those people was Marci.

"C'mon!" she said, "there's an after-party behind the stage." She led the way backstage, bumping no one, with me immediately behind her, bumping everyone.

Backstage, Marci introduced me to Billy Corgan, the band's lead singer. I tried telling him that I had just worked with him the previous night on *Saturday Night Live* and had loved the concert. Instead, I blithered until I realized I sounded like every drunken idiot who had ever wasted his time after a show.

I started jogging out of Roseland, thinking that the faster I exited, the faster everyone would forget I was there. The place was now completely empty and all the lights were on. The floor was littered with shoes from people who had removed them and thrown them at the band during the show. A few of these morons were on their hands and knees rooting around on the floor with one shoe on looking for its match. They looked like they'd had a great time that night and dying never even crossed their minds.

That's when the lyrics from the Smashing Pumpkins song "Cherub Rock" hit me: "Freak out/give in. It doesn't matter what you believe in/be someone's fool." That was the game I had to play this year as a rookie, and next year would be different.

As the shows ticked by in my first year, bands came and went, sometimes matching my mood with their music, other times with their actions. Sounding more like old KISS than Pearl Jam, Stone Temple Pilots explained that my feelings were based on the weather inside 30 Rock. Spade had once joked that he liked Stone Temple Pilots better the first time around—when they were called Pearl Jam. When lead singer Scott Weiland and the band got on the elevator with me, Weiland looked at me and asked, "Where's Spade?" I told him that I didn't know. "If you see him," he said in a mischievous, we're-gonna-kick-his-ass way, "tell him that we're looking for him." No matter how fed up I was with the show, I felt that we were all in it together. I turned to Weiland and said, "I guess we'll all choose our sides, won't we."

UB40 and Crash Test Dummies performed. As UB40 played a song I had never heard before, Al Franken was standing next to me eating what I'm sure was a pencil-flavored cookie. "I feel like I'm watching the lounge band at a Dublin Holiday Inn," he said. He was right. They were awful.

Crash Test Dummies also stunk up the joint with a cut from their album *God Shuffled His Feet* (off to the record store to return that album). Maybe I was judging on a curve. It's tough to precede Aretha. All I knew was the name and the chorus of the song they were playing, which was "mmmmmmmm." I wasn't buying it. Aretha was coming in a week and these guys could *mmmmm-mmm* their asses back to Canada.

Aretha was given time for three songs rather than the traditional two. She was amazing, but what a look. Her breasts were unlike anything I had ever seen; you should be able to put a key in her rump and drive them. And her bra was architecture.

Sometimes the musical guests were just unintentional comical relief, particularly in their appearances. Billy Joel was a troll of a man; I couldn't believe how much he looked like Jackie Mason. When I saw him, the only thing that came to mind was that musicians really do get all the chicks. It was obvious why Dwight Yoakam got all the chicks—until he removed his trademark cowboy hat. His jeans were painted on and he wore ostrich skin boots and a pimpy rhinestone shirt. However, when he took off his hat, it was like Superman returning to Clark Kent. Without the hat, he looked like Clint Howard, Ron Howard's brother.

When Snoop Doggy Dogg showed up, I brought in a photo from *Spin* magazine of him dressed in blue jeans, looking hard-core, with sweat dripping from his brow, and I asked him to sign it. He wrote: "To Jay, much respect, Snoop Doggy Dogg." But he was so high he just kept on writing, covering the entire bottom half of the photo with graffiti. Maybe it was gangsta rap hieroglyphics for "You're a cool white guy."

Pearl Jam made me feel cool—period. When they

arrived near the end of my first season, Eddie Vedder walked around with a piece of luggage resembling a bag you'd see a hobo carrying. When he opened it up, it was crammed with legal-looking papers. I had promised my future sister-in-law that I would get her Vedder's autograph. All week I waited for the right time to approach him. We literally bumped into each other the evening of the show. I introduced myself to him and asked him if he could sign something for me. He replied, "No one . . . will know!" He was doing my Christopher Walken impression at me and I loved it.

Vedder smiled and asked me if I could come into the dressing room and say hi to the rest of the band, which I had no problem doing. When I walked into Pearl Jam's dressing room, Eddie Vedder announced in Walken-ese, "Look . . . who I found." The band members all launched into snippets of Walken. For the next half hour, I stayed in their dressing room doing Christopher Walken like a trained monkey.

The bassist, Jeff Ament, asked me if I played basketball. When I told him I did, he gave me his phone number at the hotel where the band was staying and said that he was registered under the name Otis Birdsong. He told me to call him the next day so we could together and shoot some hoops. I woke up but I didn't call.

It didn't matter. Pearl Jam recognized me, so the rest of the world could kiss my ass.

———

It was the next-to-last show of the year, and Chrissie Hynde was onstage performing with the Pretenders. They were playing their song and it sounded unbelievable. But Chrissie was having a difficult time with the show's still photographer, Ken. Every time he maneuvered himself into position to snap a few shots for the hallway next to photos of the Rolling Stones and the other bands who had performed over the years, Chrissie would wave her hand and shoo him away.

During the Pretenders' second set, the photographer brought out a ladder and stood on the top step, pointing his camera down at the band. In mid-lyric, Hynde pointed at him and screamed, "Fuck off!" Beleaguered, the photographer climbed down the ladder and slunk away.

The next day, the entire cast and crew filed into studio 8-H for the annual *Saturday Night Live* photo. About fifty exhausted people stood shoulder to shoulder and smiled like everything was normal. Some kneeled. As the photographer reached the top of his ladder, Adam Sandler yelled, "Hey, Ken, Chrissie Hynde just called and she said, 'Get down!' "

In that photo, every smile was genuine. Even mine.

TEN

FAKE PITCHES

Since I had become medicated, I had more time to actually be at work—not literally but spiritually. I began to notice the smallest details of my work environment. The walls were white and they didn't close in on me anymore. I began to take notes of the things around me to maybe someday write a book about my experience. I realized that the people I worked with were not sinister after all. They were all good people in an impossible situation. I was a functional person in a dysfunctional place. I wasn't sick, the show was. It was a restaurant in a great location that served food that sometimes was awful and other times glorious.

I began to notice more and more tricks that the others applied to help them get through it all. The "I'm gonna help so-and-so with his idea" was just the beginning. Day by day, night by night, I studied everyone around me. In subsequent pitch meetings I became braver and more confident. I would scan the room and pick someone I didn't get along with and then tell Lorne I was working with him on his idea. No one ever called me out. All the others probably just wondered what took me so long to catch on.

The strangest phenomenon I noticed in pitch meetings was the fake pitch. The fake pitch was an art form. If you had no ideas, you had to think of a sliver of an idea and say it out loud and the room would move on. The fake pitch took as much energy as an actual pitch, but you were relieved of the duty of having to write it up. You could also use the fake pitch if you wanted your sketch to be a surprise at read-through. Whenever someone would execute a fake pitch, everyone in the room knew it except the host. The host probably wondered what happened to that sketch at read-through, since we all giggled throughout the entire pitch, but it was never to be seen again.

Looking back, I never understood why some guys had to pitch in the first place. If a guy as brilliant as Phil Hartman didn't have any ideas, did it really matter? Of course not. The writers would put him in their sketches anyway. Sandler nicknamed Hartman "Glue," and he was. Phil Hartman could do anything, and he did so on a weekly basis. He was money in the bank. He held everything together. As long as Phil Hartman was on the show, every sketch had at least one person in it who would never let you down. Whether he was playing Sinatra or Charlton Heston or a schoolteacher or a Bond villain or Frankenstein, he executed flawlessly. I never met anyone with Hartman's versatility.

So when it was Phil's turn to pitch an idea to the host, he would always be pleasant, smile and shrug his shoulders, and comment on the pitches that had already been heard. It was understood that out of all of us, Phil Hartman was the last guy you had to worry about ideas coming out of. If he never thought of a single idea, he was still invaluable. He could do anything and we all knew it. If we were a baseball team, Phil was certainly our MVP.

Oddly, Kevin Nealon's fake pitches were as funny as everyone else's real ones. I would have given my right arm to have actual ideas like those that he was secretly presenting as fake ones. I can still remember Kevin Nealon telling one host: "You know those runaway truck ramps on the highway? Well, you live in a house at the top of one of those runaway truck ramps, and every night at dinner a semi comes crashing through your living room."

Several weeks later, I was sitting around the table with several of the writers. I had thought the runaway truck ramp pitch was funny, but it hadn't been submitted for read-through. Acting like the rookie I was, I asked what had happened to the pitch. I was met with blank stares from everyone. Aha.

Nealon was the anchor of Weekend Update, and sketch writing wasn't expected of him. The Weekend Update anchor had such enormous responsibilities— gathering the news and spinning it for the segment— that it would've been unfair to make him sit in a room and write a sketch. Regardless of how early I arrived at work, Kevin would be in his office poring over every newspaper ever printed searching for news items that he could use for Weekend Update. Nealon's fake pitches were done pro forma, whereas Norm Macdonald's were done to throw everyone off his trail.

Norm would pitch about five fake ideas in great detail, and then at read-through he would have one winner that you never saw coming. When Bob Newhart hosted the show, Norm took about ten minutes to pitch "Literally vs. Figuratively." "I've noticed that people misuse the phrase literally when they actually mean figuratively," he began. "A guy will come out of a movie theater and someone will ask him, 'How was the movie?' and he'll respond, 'I literally laughed my head off!' "

Newhart stared at Norm thinking he was finished. We all chuckled, knowing that Norm had no intention of writing his "Figuratively vs. Literally" sketch. But the giggles didn't sate Norm. He wanted to win Newhart over. What happened next was incredible.

Norm kept adding example after example of what he

meant, trying to force Bob Newhart to crack a smile. Newhart was an idol to all of us in the room, especially to the comics. Norm fought like hell. He wasn't going to be able to sleep that night if Bob Newhart didn't laugh at his fake pitch. He plodded onward: "Sometimes, someone will say I literally cried my eyes out . . . but their eyes are still in their head, you know. Or someone will get some bad news and say, 'I literally died!' But there they are talking to you because they didn't die at all. They meant figuratively, not literally, you see."

Newhart began to smile, and Norm tasted blood. Norm kept going and going until I was convinced that if this started as a fake pitch, it was now personal. Norm was going to write it, if only to prove to Newhart how funny it was. And it *was* funny. The longer he went on and on, the funnier it became. Soon we were all in hysterics. Norm felt satisfied with himself.

That week at read-through, Norm had one sketch on the table that made it onto the show. It was Norm as Charles Kuralt. I was literally blown away.

I returned to the doctor a week after our first meeting. Since seeing her, I felt great. I walked through the emergency room of the hospital to the elevators. All around me were people in wheelchairs and on gurneys. Some of them groaned. They were dying; I wasn't.

By this time, I had become a quick study in panic disorder. *Merriam-Webster's Collegiate Dictionary* defines *panic* as "A sudden overpowering fright . . . a sudden unreasoning terror accompanied by mass flight. Synonym: Fear." Most people who believe they've had a panic attack are suffering from anxiety. Alternatively, the dictionary definition of the word *anxiety* is "Painful or apprehensive uneasiness of mind, usually over an impending or anticipated ill. Synonym: Care." The key word in distinguishing *panic* from *anxiety* in these definitions is *over*. Anxiety is over something: Your boss is an asshole, you can't pay your bills. These are things you have anxiety over. In the definition of panic, the word *over* is replaced by *unreasoning*. The synonyms for anxiety and panic are virtual opposites. Panic equals fear; anxiety equals care.

The doctor asked me how the Klonopin had been working for me. I told her it had worked like I prayed it would, only better. She told me that Klonopin was a drug developed to stop seizures in epileptics, and that it was a smart drug. This meant that if the patient didn't suffer from seizures, it redirected itself to stop the flood of adrenaline and endorphins that cause panic. If you suffered from neither malady, it would put you to sleep for a while. When she asked me if, in addition to panic, I had been suffering from depression, I responded with an offhanded "I wish." Sternly she told me, "No you don't."

She went on to say that if I wasn't suffering from depression or having any more panic attacks, that we should continue with the minimal dosage and I might want to start practicing some desensitization exercises. For example, if you were afraid of water, you could gradually work your way toward a pool and eventually put your toes in, then your feet, and so on to overcome your phobia. Considering my phobia was the place where I worked, I didn't see this as something I would have to work very hard on.

The doctor also told me that if I did cocaine or smoked pot I should stop, because both drugs induced panic. I had never even seen cocaine before in my life, let alone snorted it; however, I had been smoking pot every day for three years. I thought that marijuana was helping me with my panic attacks by mellowing me out, but I had actually been encouraging panic with each toke. Once I weighed the consequences, the decision to quit smoking pot was quick and easy. I knew then and there that I would rather have pneumonia once a month for the rest of my life than have one more panic attack.

She also explained to me the irrational nature of panic disorder. People say that when they have a panic attack their heart races and they feel like they are going to pass out, but she explained that you pass out when your heart slows down, not when it speeds up. She stood up from her desk, opened her office door for me, and said good-bye.

I asked her what time my appointment was next Monday. In a very matter-of-fact tone, she told me that she didn't need to see me again until the prescription ran out. I was stunned. I thought I'd see her every week and give her progress reports.

"You have a sickness, and we have found the right medicine for it," she explained. "You are no different from someone who walked in here with asthma and got an inhaler. You were sick, and now you're better." Then she said something I thought was really cool. "I don't see a need for you to come in here every week and tell me about your childhood."

The door was open, but I was reluctant to leave. I felt safe being near her. "What about when I fly? What if I get a panic attack in the air?" I asked.

The doctor furrowed her brow. "If your issue is structure, which we have decided and agreed it is, why would you panic on an airplane? Compared to the rest of your life, flying is the most structured thing you do. You know weeks in advance when you should wake up for your flight. The airline hands you a ticket with a seat assignment on it. If you read the monitors in the airport, they tell you what time your flight is scheduled to leave, what gate it will be leaving from, and how long it takes to get there." She was right. "If you're on a flight and you feel some symptom of panic creeping in just reach into your pocket and take an extra pill of Klonopin," she continued. "You're taking only a milligram a day. I have patients who take twenty. If you took an extra half-milligram, you're still taking a very small dosage."

That was it. I was on my own. She didn't want to peruse my childhood. I had felt for so long that I was absolutely going crazy, and it turned out I was sick. Not dying, just sick. And now I was treated and feeling fantastic. On the elevator down to the emergency room, I reached into my backpack and took out my bottle of Klonopin. I picked out two pills and put them in the small square pocket of my jeans above my right leg. My Klonopin pocket. Just in case.

Shortly after seeing the doctor, I started liking pretty much everyone. Ellen was still asshole Ellen and Schneider was still hit-or-miss, but my feelings toward everyone else became muted. Whatever mess I was in, I started to realize that I wasn't the only one. I was no longer terrified by the thought of having a panic attack, so I began speaking more.

The more I spoke to my coworkers, the more the subject of panic worked its way into the conversations. Melanie Hutsell told me she once had a panic attack that was so severe she had to be taken to the hospital, and as a result, her face froze for a few days. Spade also told me he had gone to the hospital once, and then I noticed that Spade had to have pizza and an Amstel Light at 9:00 P.M. every Saturday night—not 9:01 P.M. or 8:59 P.M., but precisely nine o'clock—or he would pass out. I also noticed that Norm Macdonald had what appeared to be a Klonopin pocket of his own. Everyone had gone through something. I wasn't alone.

It was incredible to sit in someone's office and share horror stories. Although I was no longer having panic attacks, I still had vivid memories of how crippling they were. The thought of "what if?" was always in the back of my mind. The thought I had much more of was "Why can't I enjoy this?" I didn't have anyone to blame. I never blamed myself. I never blamed Lorne Michaels. How could I? All he did was give me a chance.

Jason Patric hosted. So did Patrick Stewart and Helen Hunt. Blind Melon performed and I got high at the wrap party with Shannon Hoon, who has since overdosed and died. Sara Gilbert came through with Counting Crows. All of these shows run together for me because I wasn't in any of them.

When I wasn't on the show, I just kept drinking and drinking. I kept leaving halfway through the show on Saturdays. I kept skipping Good-nights. I wasn't on the John Goodman show, either. The final episode of my first season Heather Locklear was the guest, and she was game for anything. Fred Wolf wrote a "Home Shopping Network" sketch for her, in which she was selling blenders and saying such lines as "It's so easy even a Mexican can use it," "At this price you couldn't get it cheaper off a drunken Indian," and "Why not buy two in case a Puerto Rican steals it?" The phone lines were lighting up after every line she spoke.

I had only one line on the Heather Locklear episode, but I didn't care because finally it was over. I was in a *Melrose Place* sketch playing the gay guy. I walked into the scene and said, "That's me. Gotta go!" And off I went.

The previous August, I was shoved headfirst into a tunnel and began the struggle. The more I struggled, the more everything tightened up around me. The walls, the elevators, my rib cage, my arteries—they all constricted with each passing week. But on the night of May 14, I came out the other end of the tunnel and saw the sun.

I breathed deep on my way to the final wrap party of the year. A few of my friends had attended the final show, and I decided to bring them along. One by one, they put their arms around me and said things like, "You made it!" Not "Congratulations" or "Great job," just you made it— like a soldier returning from war. In fact, there was nothing to congratulate me on. I hadn't really done anything except survive.

The day after the final show, I boarded a plane for Los Angeles. For the first time in twenty weeks, I had nothing to worry about. I didn't have to worry about sketches or fake pitches or who liked me. I didn't have to worry about panic or anxiety. I didn't have to worry about being too early or coming in too late. My first year on *Saturday Night Live* was over, and I wasn't a rookie anymore. All I had to do was rest for a few months and return refreshed.

I spent that summer with my girlfriend, Nicole, who is now my wife. I spent day after day on the beaches and night after night in the bars. I was renting a nice house in the Hollywood Hills and bought myself a Mustang convertible. I would drive for hours with the radio blasting louder than Joe Dicso could talk, and I slipped into a calm midsummer languor.

I did more stand-up than I ever had in my life. I would perform at a Laundromat if there was a microphone. Onstage, I found no politics. I would say something and the audience would either laugh or they wouldn't. I finally had the mike back in my hand. At *SNL,* I couldn't get the mike, and when I did, it was pinned to my suit jacket and I was allowed to speak only one line. After my shows, I would sit with the other comics and get bombed. No matter what city I was in or who I was around, the conversation always turned to *Saturday Night Live.*

Comics would ask me what it was like and I didn't know what to say. I would plaster on a fake smile and tell them it was fantastic. That's what they wanted to hear. I couldn't possibly tell them everything. And if I started to tell them anything other than that it was fantastic, I found myself rambling on and on until they were sorry they asked.

That summer I also heard stories about myself and the things I had done at 30 Rock, many of which I had long since blocked out. People would ask me if it was true that I threw my phone out the window. I would have to stop and think before I answered. Yes, I did throw my phone out the window, but how did they know?

It had happened on a Tuesday night and I couldn't get anyone to help me with a sketch. I felt a surge of panic but couldn't leave my office because I would have had to run past the rest of the staff in the writers' room. So I picked up the phone on my desk and threw it through a window, which was unfortunately closed. Glass flew all over the place, and Mike Shoemaker dashed into my office to see what caused the shattering noise.

An hour later the police arrived. The telephone had landed with a good crash seventeen stories below on the street in the middle of Rockefeller Center, and the good citizens of New York had reported it. I stood in front of the phone-shaped hole in the window and told the cops someone must have broken into my office and thrown the phone out the window. I remember telling them, "I wouldn't do something like that! I talk on the phone all the time." I peered out through the window down onto the street. "Who the fuck would do something like this?!" I said. "We're just lucky nobody got hurt down there."

The cops looked out the window, too, and the three of us stood there with our heads out the window. Eventually they thanked me for the help with their investigation and left. I asked them if there was anything I could do to help them with the case. Both officers shot me a look that could only be interpreted as "Yeah, don't throw your phone out the window anymore."

No one asked me about sketches I had performed or the segments I had written. If my contribution to the show came up in conversation, it was always because I was the one who brought it up. But the people out in California asked me about Farley. They wanted to know if it was true that we wrestled in front of Alec Baldwin and the rest of the cast. Yes, we did, but how did they find out?

I didn't bring these memories to California with me, but the more conversations I had, the more they came back to me. I remembered the great stories that Alec Baldwin told, like how he stopped eating meat. He and Kim had been in Paris and he contracted food poisoning from steak. He said that he was sick for so long that he decided eating meat wasn't worth it. His story about being with Kim Basinger in Paris led me to ask what it was like to be married to the hottest woman alive. Though he assured me it was great, Alec said, "If I had to do it all over again, I would have fucked every single woman I ever came into contact with." He detailed who that crop would have been: "To all the girls Stephen and Billy brought home, I would have said, 'Come over here,' and I would have had my way with them because I was famous and I could have. Even second cousins. I would have had no morals because once you're married, it's done."

I thought about when Nancy Kerrigan hosted and

how she had a mouth like John Elway's. She had this enormous set of choppers that made her look like a whale when her mouth was open. If you held her in the ocean by her feet, she could probably filter brine shrimp from the water using her teeth. She was nice, but I don't think she was the sharpest knife in the cutting block because she gleefully signed the *Sports Illustrated* cover with the picture of her crying and clutching her knee and the headline reading " 'Why? Why? Why?' "

They wanted to know about when Rosie O'Donnell hosted because she was a fellow comic. Rosie came to have some fun, and she wanted to please. Unlike, say, Shannen Doherty, she was someone you *wanted* at the rewrite table throwing out ideas. I was in a "Malibu Fires" sketch with her in which she played Penny Marshall and I played Sean Penn. I rented old Sean Penn movies to master his walk. I couldn't do a great Sean Penn impression, but I had the walk down cold. Still, my line got a laugh: "Be nice to strangers because you never know when you are going to be a stranger, too."

When I retold these stories, people looked at me with big grins on their faces. They were smiling because it all sounded like so much fun. It all should have been fun, but it wasn't. With the telling of each story, I realized how many wonderful things I had experienced. But that didn't make them any more enjoyable. At least not yet. All they did was make me dread going back.

I went to New York twice that summer, both times to

visit my parents. I still couldn't rent a car, so I borrowed a friend's. My friend was in the FBI, and he told me that if I was ever pulled over, I should say he was my brother. I asked him, "What if they ask why we don't have the same last name?" And he repeated, "Just tell them you're my brother." I was pulled over twice in two days speeding down Route 80. Both times the cop handed me back my driver's license and told me to tell my "brother" hello.

Sometimes I would sleep at my parents' house, but mostly I made the commute from my apartment in New York to the suburbs of New Jersey. I made sure I never got stuck in the Lincoln Tunnel during rush hour. If there was the slightest congestion on my way to the tunnel, I would turn uptown and drive the half hour out of my way to the George Washington Bridge. At my parents', I cut the grass and trimmed the hedges. I signed autographs for the neighbors. I played Wiffle ball in the driveway. Everything was fine. People had driveways and mailboxes and screen doors. There were property lines and curbs, and dinner was at six o'clock. I talked a lot with my parents about not wanting to go back, but they never voiced an opinion; they just listened.

I went to a Yankee game with a close friend of mine who had season tickets. When we sat down at the stadium, he introduced me to most of the people in his section. During the game one of the people sitting behind us asked him if I was on television. He told them, "Yes. He's a bit player on *Saturday Night Live*." The words stung. I know he wasn't belittling me, but his statement hurt—probably because he was right. I knew right then and there that I had to go back. I had to make a difference. I never wanted to be called a bit player again. At home that night I read a quotation in the *New York Post* sports section from Penn State football coach Joe Paterno that hit home: "The will to win is important. But the will to prepare to win is vital."

I started preparing to win. I kept a notebook with sketch ideas and carried it everywhere I went. I even had pages full of fake pitches. Whether I was on a plane, at the beach, or at home, I scribbled in the notebook. The slightest kernels of ideas were written down. I had to go back.

There would be things working in my favor. I wasn't going to be the new guy anymore. I knew where the pencils were. I knew that Al Franken put them in his mouth. I had learned how to set my alarm to "you're paid to be here." I knew rewrites took all night for no reason. I knew not to give away any jokes until Wednesday. I knew that if you wanted to talk to Jim Downey, you were going to wait a long time. None of the new people knew anything about me. With ten new people, I could start a clean slate. They would all be asking me for help, and I would befriend them and get them to write with me.

But first the show needed to officially pick up the option on my contract.

———

When you're hired on *Saturday Night Live*, the contract is for five years with a network option at the end of each year. This meant they could bail out whenever they pleased. The salaries were pretty much favored nations, with all the first-year people making $5,500 per week. The second year, the salary increased to $6,000 and then continued to escalate each year, to $12,500 per week in the fifth year. In a stroke of good fortune, I had been hired as writer my first year, so I was earning an additional $1,500 writer's fee on top of my performance check. Contractually, the show had until July 1 to make a decision on renewing my option. Since my post–Yankee game revelation occurred in June, my notebooks and I had to wait for three weeks before I would know if they even wanted me back. They had to want me back! Didn't they?

On June 13, the show contacted my agent, Ruthanne Secunda, and asked for an extension on the option. They wanted until July 6 to make their decision to bring me back, and they required it in writing. When Ruthanne asked me what I wanted to do, I told her I wanted to tell them to make up their minds on or before July 1, just like it said in *their* contract. She warned me that we might not want to force their hand. If they were asking for an extension, then they obviously hadn't made up their minds yet, so why be combative? I agreed to the extension and felt even more inspired.

I would show them. If they would just let me return, I would hand in sketches every week and walk out onstage for Good-nights. I desperately wanted to go back. If everything was terrible again, at least I would know what to expect. I would deal with it. I was medicated.

On the afternoon of July 6, *Saturday Night Live* exercised my option. It was afternoon in Los Angeles and nighttime in New York. I woke up that morning knowing that I would receive an answer, but I hadn't anticipated the show taking until after dinner to give it to me. It was an already long day that seemed longer. By the time the news came, I was terrified. I knew that I didn't want to be on *Saturday Night Live* for only one year—certainly not for the year I had just gone through.

ELEVEN

FROM THE CRADLE

ERIC CLAPTON kept hugging me.

It was the first show of my second season. Clapton had an album coming out called *From the Cradle*. It was a great blues album. On it, he covered some Willie Dixon songs and other blues songs that had inspired him throughout his career. He was onstage on a Thursday afternoon doing a sound rehearsal. I walked into studio 8-H just in time to watch him play "Five Long Years." A week earlier I had seen Buddy Guy in concert in Central Park. "Five Long Years" was on Buddy's new album as well. When Clapton walked offstage after the song finished, I approached him, introduced myself to him, and shook his hand. He took my hand as if we were friends from college and it had been years since we last saw each other.

"I saw Buddy Guy play that song last week and I didn't think it could be played any better, but you did it," I said.

Clapton put his arm around my neck and started laughing. "Aw, thanks, man," he said.

"Buddy doesn't look at the chords, though," I added.

Clapton went bananas. He started laughing so loud that people across the studio were looking over to see what on earth was making Eric Clapton crack up. The guy was doubled over. He kept laughing and barely squeaking out, "You're right! You're right!"

I started to become self-conscious. Everybody was looking at us, and he just kept laughing. I didn't think what I said was as funny as he did, but he kept hugging me and telling me how right I was. I wanted to tell him that he really shouldn't find me this interesting. I wanted to say, "Dude, relax. You're Clapton!"

Eventually Eric Clapton and I broke off our embrace long enough for him to walk to his dressing room. I stood there for a moment, letting what just happened sink in.

I was woken up by a tap on the shoulder from Marci Klein. "What were you two just talking about?" she asked.

I didn't want to explain to her who Buddy Guy was or who wrote the song "Five Long Years" and how I didn't expect Clapton to react the way he did. Instead, I played it cool. I shrugged my shoulders and said, "Nothing. We were just rappin'."

I figured that if I could make Marci believe that Eric Clapton thought I was cool and that sometimes Clapton and I just talk and make each other laugh, that she might tell Lorne what a hot property I was—and that would lead to my being in more sketches. No such luck.

Marci jabbed her finger at me. "You are not allowed to ask the musical guest to be in a sketch," she chastised in her Smashing Pumpkins concert tone.

Though I assured her that wasn't the case, I don't think she believed me. Even after my summer writing binge, I was light-years from having enough sketch ideas that I could work Eric Clapton into any of them.

I truly believed that my second year on the show would be different. During our summer hiatus, I had filmed a movie entitled *Stranger Things* for Castle Rock Entertainment, Rob Reiner's production company. The movie was directed by Jason Alexander of *Seinfeld,* and he starred in it along with Joe Mantegna, Lolita Davidovich, and James Woods. By auditioning, I had landed the part of Joe Mantegna's bumbling nephew. All my scenes had funny stuff in them, and I was thrilled to finally be in my first motion picture.

It was evident early on during production that Joe, James, and I had a great chemistry for comedy, or at least I thought we did. I had the time of my life as I acted across from an Academy Award nominee and a seasoned pro. Almost every day we shot, I thought about how when the film became a blockbuster hit, people all over the country would watch *Saturday Night Live* with renewed interest because "that guy Jay Mohr is on it."

But it wasn't long before my big hit movie evaporated. The movie was edited by early fall, and I was invited to a screening at the Galaxy Theater in Hollywood. My agent warned me that the studio's holding a pre-release screening and not a premiere wasn't a good sign. The entire night was steeped in foreshadowing— beginning with my running out of gas on the way to the theater in the pouring rain.

But when Jason Alexander took the stage to introduce the film, I knew the fix was in. He was wearing a red sweater the exact color of the curtain behind him. With all the spotlights shining on him, all you could see was his head and his jeans. I leaned over to Nicole and said, "Who told him to wear the red sweater? Maybe there should have been a change of clothes in the car in case there's a red curtain in the theater. What are the odds? Maybe fifty-fifty."

Then the lights went down and the film started. Three minutes into the movie I knew it was going to be a disaster. The tone was all wrong. The music was all literally in *Seinfeld* instrumental tones. Jason and Lolita had this long courting scene in which they skirted the issue of their relationship. It lasted so long it became torturous to watch.

I had returned from summer to 30 Rock with a real swagger about the movie. Just wait until this baby hits the theaters, I thought to myself. I spent three months telling my coworkers and anyone else who would listen to keep their eyes peeled for *Stranger Things*. But even if they had their eyes peeled, it would have been difficult for them to find the film. The title was changed from *Stranger Things* to *For Better or Worse,* and the film went straight to video.

When I went back to the seventeenth floor for the first time, I felt something there I never had before: familiarity. All the tables were in the same place and all the walls were where I left them. I knew the people around me. I knew what they sounded like. I knew their personalities. I had seen them laugh, and I had seen them scream.

At the first table read, I had two sketches. One of them didn't get any laughs. It was funny in my head the night before when I had written it down and handed it in, but at the table it was dying. Lorne narrated as he always did and everyone read their parts well, but the sketch just wasn't funny. When my sketch ended, the room was quiet and everyone reached for the next sketch to read. From the table Adam Sandler shouted in a Joe Dicso impression, "Cast for Good-nights! Cast for Good-nights!" Everyone laughed, and for the first time I felt a part of everything.

By Adam's teasing me, I felt a little more accepted. To the new people, it probably looked like we were all old friends. To the old people, it was Sandler mocking one of the guys. I wasn't imagining it. Everyone was treating me a little differently. I had earned a modicum of respect. I worked hard. I was no longer on the writing staff. I had asked Ruthanne to negotiate me out of the writer's contract, and the show happily obliged. I never had to sit through rewrites again—though I did anyway. I contributed for as long as I could, which was normally until around three in the morning.

The first show of my second season was hosted by Steve Martin (and the musical guest was Eric Clapton). Neither one of my sketches was on the air, but I had a few lines in three others. The funniest was a pitch meeting at a marketing firm for a new candy bar named Nutriffic! In the sketch, Chris Elliott unveiled to the candy bar makers the new jingle that his marketing firm had written for Nutriffic! Steve Martin (playing a marketing exec) sat at a table and listened patiently as Chris brought out a barbershop quartet to sing the jingle: "Nutriffic! . . . Nutriffic! It's NUT very good!"

As one of the members of the barbershop quartet, my contribution was to sing the Nutriffic! jingle six times that night, four times during rehearsal and twice during the live show. I was supposed to sing it four times like everyone else during the show. However, I became distracted and forgot my last two "Nutriffics!" How in the hell could I forget a line that's written on cue cards, repeated several times, and has three other people singing it at the same time as me?

Simple. At the very end of the sketch rehearsal, as we were walking offstage to the applause of the rehearsal audience, Chris Elliott leaned into me and asked, "Did you check out Steve Martin's piece? He has the best hairpiece in show business."

No, I hadn't seen Steve Martin's hairpiece. I had seen his head with what appeared to be real hair on top, but I hadn't noticed a wig of any sort. It wasn't like Steve had put on a baseball cap for the sketch and then had the cap with the hair in it fall at my feet. Was Chris messing with me? It couldn't be a hairpiece, could it?

This burning question gnawed at me throughout the meeting in Lorne's office between dress rehearsal and air. Then I asked other cast members if Steve Martin wore a wig. No one would commit one way or the other, but the tension was heightened by several who asked if I had ever seen his hair a different style or length. No, in fact, I hadn't.

When the live show aired, I stood to the side of Steve Martin as I sang the Nutriffic! song. Steve never looked at me during the sketch, so I had free rein to stare at his head for as long as we were on the stage together. I stared at Steve Martin's head so hard I could have burned a hole into his skull. Under the hot stage lights Steve began to perspire slightly, and a few beads of sweat trickled down the side of his neck. I continued to examine his head for any sign of a wig. I looked for creases and seams, staples and netting, or traces of glue. I stared until I heard the applause signaling that the sketch was over—which meant that I had stared right through two of my four lines of the week.

To this day, I have no idea if Steve Martin wears a wig, but I still have never seen his hair a different length or style.

People always ask me how cutthroat it was on the show, and I always honestly say it really wasn't. There were many cliques, but they were easygoing and friendly ones. I never fell into one particular clique. I would visit all of them, but I never felt comfortable with any of them for very long. It was a lot like high school for me. Friends with everyone, but not really friends with anyone.

The funnest one to visit was Sandler, Spade, Farley, and Herlihy, who gathered in Sandler's office. They would all sit around and make phone calls to the girls who had written them asking them to go the senior prom. Sandler would dial the phone and ask, "Is Lucy there?" Lucy would get on the line and Sandler would say, "Lucy, it's Adam Sandler," which was followed by screaming. Sandler would then explain kindly and diplomatically that he couldn't accept her invitation to the prom because of the workload at *Saturday Night Live.*

These conversations would end with something along the lines of "Oh, I appreciate that a lot. Well, we're working hard. Okay, talk to you later."

When I was hired for the show, I came on board with Dave Attell, Sarah Silverman, and Norm Macdonald. When Spade, Schneider, and Sandler were hired for the show, they all came on board together. They had been through all the bullshit with one another as a group. Whenever I spent time with them, I felt like a freshman walking home with a group of seniors. You're in the conversation, but not really.

While I was growing up, all my friends were two years older than me. We were really tight until they went to high school and I stayed in middle school. They entered a new world of different sports practices and new friends. Consequently, we didn't have much in common. As my relationships with the older kids faded, a new kid who was two years younger than me moved in next door. I befriended him, as well as all of his friends. Then I had clout with a whole new group of kids because I was older. I was the one who had been there and done that.

My second season on *Saturday Night Live,* I employed a similar strategy. The show had hired Chris Elliott, Morwenna Banks, Janeane Garofalo, and Mark McKinney as new cast members, Molly Shannon and Laura Kightlinger as featured performers, and a few new writers. For all they knew, I was a normal guy. Michael McKean had come aboard near the end of my first season, so he wasn't part of my initial traumatic adjustment experience either. The two of us hit it off particularly well, and he was a sliver of sanity for me at *SNL*.

Michael McKean's pedigree was almost as impressive as he was personally. He had played Lenny on *Laverne & Shirley* and starred in the cult film *This Is Spinal Tap*. Mike was one of the good guys. He had a real warm, easygoing vibe about him; he was always approachable. With him, everything was simple. He would invite me to lunch on a Sunday by saying, "Hey, me and my fiancée are going to lunch. Meet us on the corner of Bleecker and Tenth near the sandwich place at noon, and we'll have a great time." I would arrive at the appointed time; he would be there, and we would have a great time, eating, laughing, and talking about everything except the show.

Most important, for whatever reason, he always listened to me. I would sit in his office and bitch about something, and he'd agree that it sucked. Then he would either pick up his guitar and sing some songs or tell me a horror story of his own that had absolutely nothing to do with *Saturday Night Live*, and we'd laugh our asses off for an hour. I finally had someone I could complain to, and he was a godsend. In hindsight, he must have been a saint because I spent a lot of time whining on the couch in his office, while he just listened.

Either because he liked me or because I complained about my lack of airtime, McKean threw me a nice bone when Damon Wayans hosted, and he did it right in the middle of rehearsal. The sketch involved Wayans as Babyface, Sandler as Tom Jones, and McKean as Tony Bennett. Halfway through rehearsal, Mike walked off the set and over to me. "Can you do Tony Bennett?" he asked. I had never tried a Tony Bennett impression, so I did one on the spot for him. "You should do it in this sketch because I'm not really nailing the impression," he said. I told him I was fine with that. McKean then walked over to Lorne and simply said, "Jay's gonna do Tony Bennett. He does the impression better than me." Lorne nodded, and Mike headed for his dressing room.

On one day that I was feeling particularly down, Mike lifted my spirits with a story about the time he ate a brick of hash. It happened during the European press tour for *This Is Spinal Tap*. On this particular day, Mike related, the cast was flying from Hamburg to London and one of them was holding a brick of hash. Not wanting to waste it or risk being busted at customs, McKean ate the whole thing.

When the cast arrived in London, it was madness. There was a three-hour line for media to get into the press room to interview them. But as he was disembarking from the plane, Mike realized that he could not speak a word of English. "I was speaking gibberish," he explained to me. Gibberish? "I would say, 'Abba, bo, bo, gigi, gaga.' But in my mind, I knew what I was saying, so I sat there for seven hours answering questions in gibberish. They would ask a question, and I would answer, 'Laka, laka, choo, choo,' and the entire room would burst into laughter. No one knew I was actually in another dimension."

The brilliant part was that Mike was so high that he had an actual language in his head, and he was repeating words that meant the same thing to him as the first time he said them an hour ago, causing the reporters to nod and say, "Oh, the laka, laka thing again." The whole thing was a parody of a guy who was blotto—but he really *was* blotto.

I still can't eat corn chowder because of McKean. My second season a big bunch of us did a sketch about cops who can't stop vomiting at a crime scene. It started with Mike and me (dressed as cops) arriving on the scene of a murder. Upon viewing the body, we begin projectile-vomiting all over each other. The crew had rigged tubes that ran up our backs and out the ends of our sleeves. The tubes came out the backs of our coats, across the floor, and into the source of the vomit, which was several giant barrels of corn chowder. The vomit tubes were something of an inexact science. Ideally, whenever we put the tubes up to our mouths, corn chowder would spray out of our sleeves on cue. The problem was that some of the tubes worked and some didn't.

Cast members would be in the middle of saying their lines and corn chowder would come rocketing out of their sleeves, which were still at their sides. Thinking fast, we would immediately lift our sleeves alongside our mouths—only to have the "vomit" stop. It was priceless live television. Though the tubes worked on cue a couple of times, for most of the sketch we were at their mercy. By the end of the sketch, there were about ten people onstage stopping in mid-sentence to quickly put their sleeves up to their faces, and the motion of moving our arms from our sides to our faces was inadvertently spraying vomit all over the person next to us.

During the sketch, the smell of corn chowder became so strong that I started to gag. I wasn't alone. I looked at the others, whose eyes were watering and throats were quivering. The audience could plainly see that the tubes were operating erratically and at the wrong time. The sketch became a backdrop to the fact that we were all laughing in the middle of our lines as corn chowder shot all over the stage and all over us.

When it was over, we were all covered in what had become the most disgusting substance on earth. Cue cards and protocol went out the window during that sketch. It was such madness that if I had *actually* vomited, I don't think anyone would have noticed. That night was an example of how wonderful *Saturday Night Live* could be, and it was absolutely some of the most fun I had on the show. The audience was being treated to a sketch within a sketch, and the cast was all in the corn chowder together.

TWELVE

DRESSING DOWN

IT WAS the first Thursday of the new season and I was on my way to studio 8-H to rehearse a sketch. Since I had some extra time, I figured I would first stop by my dressing room and feng shui the place. But when I reached my previous year's dressing room, the door said CHRIS ELLIOTT on it.

I was confused at first, then relieved. Maybe I had been moved to one of the larger dressing rooms. Most everyone else had the same dressing rooms as the year before, but some of the dressing rooms were reassigned to accommodate the new cast members. I was obviously one of the people that had to move to a new dressing room—though no one actually ever told me my dressing room would be moved. Just as in my rookie days, I found out by mistake. But because of the way the network had handled my option, I was happy just being back working on the seventeenth floor at 30 Rock—let alone being on camera, even if it was for only a few sentences at a time.

I went looking for Marci Klein to find out where I would be spending my next twenty Saturdays. I found her in the conference room outside of Lorne's ninth-floor office. When I asked her where my new dressing room was, she told me it wasn't ready yet. When I asked her when it would be ready, she told me she didn't know.

Since you're not supposed to be in wardrobe until Saturday, I didn't really need a dressing room that night at all. On Thursdays and Fridays, it was more a place to hang out and wait around. You could excuse yourself from rewrites early and go down to your dressing room and read a book for an hour until your sketch came up. I didn't have a book or a dressing room, so I wandered around the halls.

I noticed that there were new photos up from the previous year. Unlike in the past, the photos were memories, not devices for intimidation. I saw photos of Nicole Kidman with Mike Myers, Emilio Estevez with Rob Schneider, and Charlton Heston standing on stage during Good-nights. I remembered Sandler doing an impression behind closed doors of the way Charlton Heston shuffled his feet when he walked. We had to keep in mind Mr. Heston's age when we submitted sketches that week. He was pretty old. There weren't going to be any pratfalls on the air that show.

On the Heston show, a "Planet of the Apes" sketch was scheduled to run during the opening monologue. The show had hired fifty extras to play apes, and the wardrobe department had secured the actual uniforms from the *Planet of the Apes* movies. The basic premise of the sketch was that the show, to Charlton Heston's horror, had been overrun by apes. The makeup department put several cast members and all the extras in perfect ape makeup. The process of being made up to look like an ape took five hours. I told anyone and everyone that there was no way I could be an ape, so I played a slave of the apes. (What if I had a panic attack under all that ape makeup?) Dave Attell had to be an ape. Attell was a chain smoker, but he couldn't reach his lips with a cigarette through the ape mask. It was easy to know which ape was Dave because he was the only ape with a five-inch cigarette holder sticking out of his mouth. Christopher Walken was right, after all; ape suits are funny.

During rehearsal of the "Planet of the Apes" sketch, Heston slapped Farley down pretty good. Farley, along with Phil Hartman, Melanie Hutsell, and me, was playing a slave, and he was getting bored, so he started mumbling, "I'm a slave, I just beat my dick all day." Then he whipped it out and actually started masturbating. Though we were all in a cage about forty feet from Heston, the man who will always be Moses to me saw what was happening and yelled in that biblical-sounding voice, "Knock it off!" Farley was so shocked that he quickly scooted it back into his pants. "I'm sorry, Mr. Heston," Chris said sheepishly.

The night of the ape sketch, I stayed for Good-nights. The musical guest on that show was Paul Westerberg, who had been the lead singer of the Replacements, one of the truly great American bands. They had split up and now Westerberg was going it solo. We were all excited and honored to have him. It seemed as though everyone was a fan—except Mr. Heston. When we all gathered onstage at the end of the show, Charlton Heston announced: "I would like to thank Paul Westerfield!" Paul Westerberg leaned over and whispered a correction into Mr. Heston's ear. Charlton Heston looked back into the camera and bellowed, "Excuse me. Paul Westerfield!" Like I said, he was pretty old.

I continued scanning the photos on the wall and slowly began to realize there was something missing from all the pictures: me. Photograph after photograph had cast members and hosts and musical guests for last season. No matter how hard I looked, I couldn't find myself in any of them—because I wasn't *in* any of them.

Slightly baffled, I rode the elevator back up to the seventeenth floor to see if any new photos were hanging in the hallway. Sure enough, there were, but I wasn't in any of them. There was no recorded history on the walls of my ever having been on *Saturday Night Live*. I even saw photos of sketches that had been cut and were never on the air hanging on the wall. I looked for me as

Christopher Walken with Jeff Goldblum. I looked for me as Andrew McCarthy with Christian Slater. I looked for me as Sean Penn with Rosie O'Donnell. As far as the walls were concerned, none of it had ever happened.

By the time I returned to the studio, rehearsals had reached the midway point. They had started without me (as they should have). When asked where I had been, I replied that I was in the bathroom. I wasn't going to start the first show of my second season complaining about not being represented on the walls. The only people who ever saw those photos were the host, the cast, and the writers. I decided to let it go and concentrate on putting my face where it meant a lot more to me—on television.

Dress rehearsals are a pretty boring affair. The cast assembles on the set and runs through each sketch from beginning to end to allow director Dave Wilson to choreograph the camera movements. There's nothing artistic about it, because every few steps Dave's voice booms out "Hold it!" over the loudspeaker system. The cast freezes and Dave pushes a different button in the control room and communicates over the headsets to all of his cameramen. He would tell which camera to shoot from what angle. Each step could take anywhere from five seconds to five minutes at a time.

The most amusing dress rehearsal was when the show installed new cameras. During the entire dress rehearsal, there were about fifty Japanese guys in suits watching the cameras operate. It was, Hey, look at our shiny new Toyotas doing laps around the speedway. It was surreal. Just when you are trying to find a groove, the audience is composed of fifty men who don't speak English and have their backs to the stage.

Rehearsals, however, were always the best time to shoot the bull with the other cast members. During the breaks, everyone would crack jokes and tease one another. If your rehearsal had either Farley or Sandler in it, you were always in for a good time. Sandler would tell these incredible stories. One of my favorite Sandler stories was the one he told us about the time that Mr. Belvedere sat on his own balls.

Adam had a small guest part on the show *Mr. Belvedere* early in his career. On his first day, everyone was sitting at a huge table waiting to start the read-through of that week's show. The old guy who played Mr. Belvedere hadn't shown up yet, so everyone was drinking coffee and talking until he arrived. Finally Mr. Belvedere walked in, looking very gay in a sweatsuit and with a matching monogrammed attaché case. When the old guy took his seat, he sang out "Goooood morning, everybody!" like a British Ted Baxter. As he took a load off, he apparently sat on one of his testicles. With his nut scrunched under his leg, he screamed, *"Oooooooohhhh-hhh!"* and had to be carried out on a stretcher.

Farley didn't need any stories. Just being around him

made you laugh. Even if he wasn't saying anything, I would just stare at him. I was convinced that I was looking at the greatest entertainer in the world. But when he did speak, he always seemed to come up with something funny.

Take Farley's background talk. Sometimes the beginning of a sketch called for some white noise background talk. If the sketch took place in an unruly courthouse or at a ball game, everyone would have to mutter fake dialogue until the camera settled on the first person with actual lines. Some of the extras were real actors with real training, and they would have scripted sentences that they had learned to say during this time. I always just looked at whoever was next to me and said, "So anyway, I was talking to Mathew and he . . ." I don't know why or when I picked that particular sentence, but it was my trademark blather. Farley would always belt out at the top of his lungs: "Murmur! Murmur! Spade's gay! Murmur!" I would always piss my pants when he did that and end up forgetting what sketch I was in and what lines I had.

If rehearsals were running long, Phil Hartman had a standard funny line that he would always deliver at the exact time everyone felt things were dragging. He would look up at the ceiling of the studio and yell, "You got a lot of talent out here, Davy, and they're baking in the sun!"

Phil Hartman was always nice to me. Though it was obvious that the show took a lot out of most of us, Phil didn't seem affected by any of it. Sandler, too, was another guy who never seemed to be having any problems. During my first season, I was looking through a car magazine and came across of a photo of a beautiful red Corvette. I tore it out of the magazine and asked Phil to autograph it for me. In black Sharpie, Phil scrawled "Phil Hartman USA!" across the side of the Corvette. I hung it in my office above my desk for the rest of the year, and aside from a pile of notebooks, my backpack, and a few empty coffee cups, it was the only thing in my office.

At the end of the year when I was cleaning out my office, one of my best friends, Matt Frost, was with me. I hadn't decorated the place much, so I spent most of the day throwing out old newspapers. When I reached for the Phil Hartman autograph to take it down, Matt stopped me. "You're not going to throw that away, are you?" he said. I was planning on tossing it out along with everything else and just bring home my notebooks. Matt looked at me like I was crazy. "You can't throw that away! It's good luck. You have to save it and hang it next year when you come back."

"Phil Hartman USA!" spent that entire summer in my sock drawer between two magazine pages to keep it in good shape. I brought it back to the show as my good luck charm, and this year I planned to hang it in my dressing room instead of my office. My dressing room was where I needed the most luck, because it was where I had really freaked out.

After dress rehearsal ended that first Thursday, I looked around for Marci Klein again. I was carrying the "Phil Hartman USA!" Corvette ad, which I had now been holding for a few hours. All I wanted to do was find my new dressing room and hang it on the wall for good luck. I found Marci in the conference room again and asked her if my dressing room was ready. She said it was, picked up a set of keys from the middle of the table, and led me away.

As we walked down the hall, I asked her if the reason it hadn't been ready yet was because they were having it cleaned. She didn't answer and continued walking very quickly in front of me. We reached a door that I had never noticed, and she found the corresponding key to open it. When she inserted the key to unlock the door, she cautioned, "Don't get mad. Okay?"

My heart sank. Though I had never seen the door she was about to open, I must have walked past it a hundred times. As Marci opened the door and revealed the inside of my new dressing room, I thought I was the victim of a practical joke. The room was much smaller than my old one. It was literally no more than ten square feet. I stepped inside with a stupid grin on my face. When I turned back around, Marci had left and I was alone in the tiny room.

I examined the door, which said JAY MOHR on it. As I moved the door back and forth, it brushed against the recliner inside the room. There were old paint chips on the floor and the smell of new paint was nauseating. I slowly began to realize that this was no practical joke; this was my new dressing room.

I sat down in the recliner and shut the door with my foot. There was no television. There was no sink or closet. There wasn't any room for anything except the worn-out recliner and the body sitting on it. I noticed one of the walls had a rectangle sunken into it. As I looked closer, I realized that it was an elevator door. The reason I smelled paint was because the elevator door had just been painted shut. There were paint chips on the floor because the door to my new dressing room had previously been painted shut as well. The room wasn't ready yet because someone had to chip the paint off the door so it would open. And that's why I had never seen the door before: It had been painted shut in the same color as the wall of the hallway.

My new dressing room was an old elevator shaft. I didn't think that my little box room was a fitting place for my "Phil Hartman USA!" autograph, so I brought it back upstairs to my office and hung it above my desk, the same as last year.

The night of the live show, there wasn't anywhere in the room to hang my costumes, so the wardrobe department had folded them and set them down across the recliner. I threw them on the floor and sat down. If anyone asked me why my clothes were wrinkled, I would tell them because my dressing room is a goddamn elevator shaft. I sat in the chair and stretched my arms out to see if I could touch both walls at the same time with my fingertips. I was a few inches short. I took two pencils and held them in my hands and stretched out again. With the pencils in my hands, I could write on both walls at once. So I sat there with my pencils, waiting for the show to begin, and scribbled parallel lines on the walls from my seat.

Since there was no television, I quickly grew bored with my cave drawings. I sat there in silence for a while and enjoyed the quiet. I assumed the tranquility was due to the fact that the room did not have an intercom box in it. Would someone come and get me when it was time for me to be onstage, or would I have to go outside every minute and check? As showtime grew closer and closer, my tension increased. I would always get an adrenaline rush before going onstage, but as Tom Petty once wrote, the waiting is the hardest part. So I sat in my tiny room on the recliner with my feet against the door. If anyone tried to come in unannounced, I would be able to block them from entering. Despite my surroundings, I felt fantastic. I knew that all the anxieties and nervousness I was feeling were appropriate. I was alone in the smallest room in the building with nothing except my thoughts, but at least I didn't think I was going to die.

I approached the new dressing room as a desensitization exercise. A lot of people I knew would have gone bananas in such a little room. I was feeling just a little claustrophobic. My claustrophobia wasn't what eventually drove me from the room. I don't know how long I sat there (no clock or watch), but I started to get nervous that everyone had forgotten about me. No one had knocked or stuck a head in. I could hear people standing in the hallway right outside my door talking.

Occasionally I heard people run past. They were all doing something. Why wasn't I? I had already been late for a rehearsal once that week, and knew that being late twice would make me look like a complete jackass. So I decided I would go down to the stage and see for myself what was going on. I stood up, sucked my stomach in so the doorknob wouldn't graze it, and opened the door to find myself standing face-to-face with thirty strangers.

The moment the door opened, they all turned to see who was emerging, and I could see their faces register disappointment instantly when I stuck my head out. No one in the group looked familiar to me. In fact they all looked wide-eyed and out of place. As the line of people moved past my doorway, I spotted an NBC page in a blue blazer bringing up the rear. The people outside my door were in a tour group. They were walking through the hallowed halls of *Saturday Night Live* listening to tidbits of history about the show. I'm sure everyone in the tour group had been hoping from the moment they stepped inside the building to see one of the show's stars. They got me instead. I felt like an animal in the zoo.

I stood there to see how many of the tourists recognized me. I still had the pencils in my hand, making me fully prepared in case any of them asked me for my autograph. I positioned myself directly underneath the JAY MOHR sign on the door and tried to make eye contact with all of them. Thirty pairs of eyes looked back at me, but none had a flicker of recognition. Instead, they were all craning their necks to see which room I had just come out of.

As I closed the door, I angled my body so they couldn't see inside my dressing room. One by one, they went past. They all looked so expectant and hopeful, and I was trying to deliver by standing directly in front of them under a sign with my name on it. When the last of the tour group had passed, the NBC page in the blue blazer looked at me with a puzzled look on her face. She was trying to place me—or so I thought. Once she put one and one together and figured out who I was, she would probably point me out to the tour group and I would be stuck there all night signing autographs and answering questions about Farley. She pointed behind me, no doubt reading the name on the door and figuring it all out. "Has that door always been there?" she asked.

I told her it had been, and then tried to be as tiny as possible and just get away from all of them. I walked a few feet down the hallway and then turned back around. I ripped the sign with my name off the door. Why advertise that you have the smallest dressing room in the history of *Saturday Night Live*?

Later in the season, I learned that my dressing room

crisis wasn't the worst ever, because at least I had a dressing room. I was bitching and moaning to everyone about it one night when Mike Myers pulled me aside. Mike told me that the size of my dressing room was indeed bullshit, but he had it much worse when he was first hired on the show. He went on to tell me that for the first two years he was on the show, he didn't have a dressing room *or* an office. Mike Shoemaker had informed him that they simply did not have any room for him, so for two years, Mike Myers sat on the floor across from the elevators with his notebooks spread out around him.

I couldn't believe it! We're talking about Mike Myers. He told me his legs cramped from sitting Indian-style for hours at a time. When I asked him if he complained to anyone, he told me that he hadn't because he was worried that he had never actually been hired. Mike apparently had never been given the welcome aboard from Marci or Mike Shoemaker or Jim Downey. Chris Farley never fake-vomited in his lap. The fact that he was forced to sit on the floor until a meeting was called or rehearsals began made him reluctant to broach the issue. He told me that after a while he figured that if the only place they had for him was on the floor across from the elevators, the next spot for him was probably out on the street.

Having gone mad my first season on the show feeling like an outcast, I was curious how Mike handled his own situation. He said that after a few weeks passed, he started bringing a tennis ball to work with him. Whenever the elevator doors opened on the seventeenth floor, Mike would throw the ball into the elevator as hard as he could so it would ricochet off the back wall of the elevator and bounce back. This version of catch was the way he worked out his frustrations. I asked him what he did when there were actually people in the elevator. Mike gave me a funny grin. "Oh, that was when it was the best!" he said.

I felt good about my conversation with Mike Myers because I was communicating with others about the show—something I was unable to do my first year. I appreciated the fact that Mike had taken the time to commiserate with me. It was somehow comforting to know that one of the show's biggest stars had gone through even more bullshit than I had.

After being inaugurated into my new dressing room, I walked back to the studio. The sketch I was in wasn't even close to being rehearsed. The camera blocking was taking longer than expected, and the cast was still rehearsing one of the first sketches in the rundown. I probably had about an hour to kill. I wasn't going to go back to my new dressing room, so I went to my old one. I was hoping that the topic of conversation being "this used to be my dressing room" would take up some of the time.

I knocked on the door that read CHRIS ELLIOTT and

there was no answer. I opened the door and Chris wasn't inside. Tim Meadows was coming out of his dressing room, so I asked him if he had seen Chris. Tim told me that he was in hair and makeup. I thanked Tim for the information, though I was really thanking him for the communication. My first year, the same question would have been met by a mumble as the person walked away from me. Tim actually looked me in the eye and gave me a straight answer.

I walked back through the halls reinspecting the walls for photos, hoping that I had missed one. I hadn't. When I got to the hair and makeup department, Chris Elliott was sitting in a makeup chair. Because he refused to shave his beard, he looked a little like a landlocked sea captain. Across from him was a dummy's head with a hairpiece on it. I leaned against the makeup counter and asked him how he liked the dressing room. He joked that it was the definition of luxurious, and I bit my tongue. I looked around the room for the owner of the hairpiece, but everyone in the chairs had full heads of hair.

"Chris, whose toupee is that?" I asked.

Very calmly he responded, "That's mine."

I was embarrassed and also immediately baffled. I had watched Chris Elliott on television for years and one thing was clear: He was slowly *losing* his hair. Whenever he appeared on *Letterman*, Chris always had a few wisps of stray hair waving off of his head. Those wisps, I discovered that night in the makeup room, were fake. The guy was brilliant! He had a hairpiece that made it look like he was losing his hair so no one would realize that he actually *was* losing his hair.

Though Chris has since dropped the lid, there was one cast member (who shall remain nameless because he's still using the hairpiece in secret) who was found out when he had a toupee mishap. It occurred at a Monday night basketball game during my second year. This particular cast member had been on the show a long time and rarely fraternized with the rest of us, but he had decided to play. He arrived with a baseball hat on his head. About five minutes into the first pickup game, he went up for a rebound and his baseball hat fell off. We were all crowded around jumping for the same rebound, so when his hat came off with his hair still in it, we gasped in horror. The guy was completely bald!

Some of the cast and writers knew this already, but even if we had all known, it still would have been mortifying. We all backed away and watched as the hat fell top side down with the hair still in the hat looking up at us. The cast member calmly bent down, picked up his hat, put it back on his head, and walked out of the gym without saying a word. After that night in the gym, whenever I saw him, I would look at his shoulders when I spoke to him so I wouldn't be tempted to stare at his hairline. And from that point on, whenever I saw him on television, I would stare at the screen and remember his entire head of hair in the baseball hat on the gym floor.

As I was standing in the makeup room talking to Chris about hairpieces, I realized that I would eventually have to go back to my room and change into my wardrobe. I dreaded going back to my room because I knew that every time I opened the door to go in or out, all the people in the show's greenroom would see me because my dressing room was directly across from it.

The greenroom was the place where the overflow of guests would be put during the show. Whenever there was a sketch that took place in the hallway, there was always a pope, three Vegas showgirls, a guy in a mule suit, two guys in a horse suit, and various and sundry paid extras. All of these characters in the hallways were directed to wait in the ninth-floor greenroom across from my elevator shaft dressing room, and because I had removed the sign, sometimes they would overflow into my private space. If a celebrity brought a dozen friends, they would watch the live show from the greenroom while the celebrity would undoubtedly be on the studio floor standing next to Marci Klein.

Unlike the people in the tour group, I didn't want anyone—not even the guy in the pontiff costume— coming out of the greenroom to recognize me. It would be humiliating. I would open a door with no nameplate on it and head inside. Everyone would turn to see who I was just in time to see me throw my clothes on the floor and push the door shut with my feet. They would all think I was on probation because I was relegated to such a small dressing room.

Finally, as nonchalantly as possible, I left Chris Elliott and his toupee behind and went back to my dressing room to change into my wardrobe. I was hoping that if anyone did recognize me, they would think that my dressing room was just a place close to the stage where I stashed some extra clothes. I picked my wrinkled wardrobe up off the floor and turned and walked out like I was on my way to someplace much larger and cooler. Now that I had my clothes and had left my dressing room, I was faced with the dilemma of where I would actually change.

I settled for a stall in the men's bathroom. There, I stripped out of my street clothes and put my sketch clothes on. Thankfully, the pants had plenty of pockets. I felt like a moron carrying my street clothes through the halls, so I went back up to my office on the seventeenth floor and left them there, a practice I followed for most of the year.

When I got off the elevators back down on the eighth floor, I could hear Joe Dicso was halfway through the casting call for the sketch I was in. Thank God for the intercom boxes, I thought to myself. Thank God for Joe Dicso and his voice.

The small space of my new dressing room had made Joe Dicso's voice even louder. Joe had been the show's stage manager since the inaugural show. He wore a headset that was connected with a wire to a sound box he wore on his belt. The box on his belt had a few buttons on it, and depending on which button he pushed, Joe could talk to the control room or the other stage manager, Bob Van Rye, who had also been a stage manager since the first show. During both rehearsals and the live show, Joe could push a button and his voice would be heard through the intercom speakers that were in the dressing rooms, as well as throughout the eighth and ninth floors. Joe was the one who told you what was next, who was in it, and how long before you had to be onstage. In some of the dressing rooms, the intercom boxes were alarmingly loud, and mine was definitely one of those.

One day after my dressing room was wired for sound, Michael McKean and his girlfriend were sitting there when Joe Dicso's voice exploded into the room: " 'Buh-Bye' will be next! 'Buh-Bye' will be next. David, Chris, Tim, Janeane, Ellen, Adam, Michael, Chris, Rob, and Jay! We are behind schedule, guys! We gotta go, we gotta go!" My dressing room was five feet by nine feet and the door was closed, so with the three of us in it the room seemed much smaller. With Joe's voice chopping us into pieces, it seemed like a prison cell.

I knew that Joe said everything twice over the intercom. The entire cast was in the "Buh-Bye" sketch, and since I knew Joe was going to say all of our names again, I looked at the door and realized it would look strange to

Michael and his girlfriend if I sprinted out of the room without explanation. McKean jumped a little and made a joke about how loud the intercom box was. Joe started to murder me. He pushed the button on his belt again and after a few seconds of feedback he belted out another rendition: "David, Chris, Tim, Janeane, Ellen, Adam, Michael, Chris, Rob, and Jay! We are behind schedule, guys! We gotta go, we gotta go!"

But McKean reached the door before I did. As he opened it and stepped out into the hallway, he looked back at me, laughing. "You know there's a big volume knob on the back of that thing," he said. I thought, Are you shitting me? My ears have been bleeding for a year and a half and you mean to tell me there's a big volume knob on the back of the speaker?

The door swung closed and I was alone in the room with Joe and his voice and the speaker box. I pulled the chair under the speaker and climbed up. I put my face against the wall sideways, so I could look at the back panel of the box. The volume knob was an inch from my face and right next to it was a bright red sticker that read VOLUME. Why hadn't I noticed this before? The knob was so big that the box had to be hung a few inches from the wall to make room for it. I grabbed the volume knob and turned it to zero. I got down from the chair and turned toward the door—happy with myself and thankful for Michael McKean—when Joe stabbed me in the back. "'BUH-BYE' WILL BE NEXT. WE GOTTA GO, GUYS!" I climbed back up behind the box on the wall. I read the sticker and studied the numbers on the dial. Joe started to read the names again and I turned the volume dial to 5, but the sound level stayed the same no matter what adjustment I made to the knob. I sprinted out of the room after all.

After rehearsing the "Buh-Bye" sketch, I stopped by the graphics department for a roll of duct tape. I spent the rest of the evening standing on my chair putting duct tape across Joe Dicso's mouth on my wall. None of the other volume knobs in the dressing rooms were broken, just mine. Duct-taping someone's mouth might be effective, but it had little effect on Joe's voice coming out of the box. His voice was just as loud as it had been. It just sounded like somebody else's. I was still being tortured every time an announcement was made, but I was glad the voice no longer sounded like Joe's, because I liked Joe.

Later in the season, I received a one-week reprieve from my elevator shaft dressing room when one of the main cast members had an illness in his family and couldn't be at the show on Saturday. To me, that meant a dressing room had just opened up. I badgered Marci Klein all week, saying that if anybody deserved to get the new dressing room, it was me. Marci agreed with me and assured me that come Saturday it would be mine.

The free dressing room was like the *SNL* presidential

suite. It was a two-person corner room with enough space for two couches and two chairs and doors on both sides. One of the walls had a long mirror encircled with bright lights running across it. The place was twice the size of my first dressing room and ten times (no joke) the size of my new tiny one.

On Saturday, Marci kept her word and handed me the keys to the corner dressing room with the two doors. I put my backpack on the floor and started shadow-boxing. I had so much room that I could have jumped rope and jogged. I sat on both couches and measured them up against each other. Which one was I going to sit on all day? I had asked out of another courtroom sketch in which I played another speechless bailiff. Since I wasn't in any other sketches, I had planned on watching golf with the lights off and sleeping until the show was over. I took off my shoes and lay on the winning couch to settle in. I was drifting off to sleep when there was a knock on one of the doors.

Marci was in the hallway outside my door standing with *Beverly Hills 90210*'s Brian Austin Green, who had a walk-on part on the show, and Tiffani-Amber Thiessen, his girlfriend at the time. Marci introduced the three of us and informed me that they would be sharing the dressing room. We all shook hands and then Marci walked out of the dressing room and shut the door behind her. The dressing room didn't look so big anymore.

The three of us sat in uncomfortable silence for a few

minutes. Finally, Brian asked me if he could change the music on the boom box that I had brought to work that day. The CD that was playing was Miles Davis's *Kind of Blue*. I asked him if he was serious and informed him that it was one of the greatest albums ever made. Brian Austin Green looked at me and said, "I only listen to rap." Great. I was no longer spending the evening alone, napping in a giant dressing room and listening to jazz. I was now sharing a dressing room with two teen idols who took over my radio and played rap all night. I like rap a lot, but the fact that Brian Austin Green was picking which songs we were listening to was torture.

My evening was ruined until I started thinking about how much it must have sucked for Brian Austin Green. This poor guy flies from L.A. to New York to have a walk-on part on *Saturday Night Live*. It's such a big deal that he brings his celebrity girlfriend with him, but when he arrives at the show and everyone is finished kissing their asses, they get shoved in a dressing room for three and a half hours with someone they had never met. They were both very polite about the whole awkward situation of sharing a dressing room with a guy who didn't need one. Episodes like this didn't bother me much. I just wanted to get on camera.

"GOOD MORNING, BROOKLYN"

GETTING YOUR *legs broken* was a euphemism my manager and I used to describe what it was like not having a sketch on the show. It was appropriate because when I wasn't in anything, I felt like I could hardly walk. The most painless way to get your legs broken was not to have anything picked for the show on Wednesday night. If Lorne's corkboard didn't have an index card with your sketch, you knew right away that you were shut out and it was time to start drinking heavily.

Sometimes it wasn't until Thursday night rehearsals that the sledgehammer hit you. Perhaps the show was running long and your sketch had to be removed from the rundown so the show would stay on time. The bad news could also find its way to you on Friday night. If you were still in the game on Saturday, you still had to clear the live dress rehearsal at 8:00 P.M. before the 11:30 P.M. live show. Even after the live dress rehearsal, something always had to go.

An hour before the show, everyone would wait outside Lorne's ninth-floor office for the final verdict. We all knew that no matter what happened, at least two sketches would be removed from the corkboard and thumbtacked to the side. No one spoke much during this time. Too much was on the line, and everyone was a little nervous, always knowing how arbitrary the process was. Sometimes the funniest sketch would be cut. I don't know why, but it happened regularly. Even if your sketch survived the live dress rehearsal, it could still be bumped if the show started to run long.

On "Good Morning, Brooklyn," my legs got broken not with a snap, but slowly and gently, which was even more painful. I first pitched "Good Morning, Brooklyn" when Marisa Tomei hosted, which was the second show of my second year. She seemed like a real nice gal. When I said hello, she said hello back. With memories of how my first year had ended still fresh in my head, I needed no more. Say hello back to me and you were forever cool.

"Good Morning, Brooklyn" was perfect for Marisa Tomei. It was basically a parody of *Regis and Kathie Lee,* but with Italian hosts and the show set in Brooklyn, with all the guests being people from the neighborhood. My character, the host of "Good Morning, Brooklyn," was named James Barone, and his cohost was Angela Tucci. I was particularly pleased with myself in naming the characters because James Barone was actually a classmate of mine in high school. We had remained friends, so I derived great pleasure knowing that he was about to be immortalized on television—assuming the sketch didn't get cut.

The sketch generated huge laughs from the normally tough crowd, both when I pitched it on Monday and then again at read-through on Wednesday after Steven Koren, a writer, and I fleshed it out. I felt good about its chances because it passed the *SNL* litmus test. Rule number one: Make the host funny. Marisa had several zingers in "Good Morning, Brooklyn." Rule number two: Put the female cast members in your sketch. I had written parts for Molly Shannon and Janeane Garofalo, and made sure they would get laughs as well.

I waited around the writers' room while Lorne, the producers, and Marisa decided if "Good Morning, Brooklyn" would make the cut. For an hour and a half they deliberated behind closed doors. None of it bothered me. I waited like everyone else and felt no anxiety. Everyone knew the sketch was hilarious, and they knew that I knew. It was almost assumed that my sketch would be chosen. After everyone got to know each other a little better during my first season, we started hanging around together after read-through, trying to predict which sketches would be picked for air. We were pretty successful.

Mike Shoemaker, one of the producers, announced to us that the door was going to open soon, so we all walked to Lorne's office and milled around the wall with the letters, which was in front of the half-dozen secretaries stationed outside his office. When the door opened I was reading a protest letter from a guy who was appalled that we used the word *nut* over and over again. I never read where the guy lived because the wind from the door caught all the letters, blowing them up into the air, leaving them desperately clinging to their thumbtacks. I turned from the wall, walked into Lorne's office, and at the top of the first column of the corkboard was a yellow index card that read GOOD MORNING, BROOKLYN.

Oddly, I didn't feel particularly elated. I knew it deserved to be up there. I walked back to my office and a few people patted me on the back and offered congratulations. When I saw Steve Koren, he was beaming. "First sketch!" he called out, stretching his hand up for a high five. Being first was a big deal because it meant that we had written the funniest sketch of the week. I instinctively walked to the phone to tell my friends that there was a reason for them to watch the show. Shortly into my first season, I had stopped calling because whenever my sketch was cut, the first question they asked when I saw them was "What happened?" But because "Good Morning, Brooklyn" was scheduled to lead the show, I decided that it was safe to spread the word.

JAY MOHR

After I had finished calling everyone—except my parents, who had long since gone to bed—I walked back toward Lorne's office. I was going to see if Marisa Tomei was still around so I could thank her. I found her in Marci Klein's office, reintroduced myself, and told her how much fun we were going to have. She was very engaging and bright, and we chatted for ten minutes or so. But the conversation took a turn when she asked me how long I had been a cast member.

Without sounding the least bit defensive, I explained that I wasn't a cast member yet, I was still a featured performer. Her face dropped. "You're not even a cast member?" she said, half as a question, half as a statement. It became obvious that she didn't want to talk to me anymore. Her answers grew shorter and she stopped making eye contact with me. I said good night to her and went home, carrying with me a funny feeling that it was best I hadn't awakened my parents.

When I arrived on Thursday night for rewrites, Jim Downey pulled me aside. I was about to learn how many different ways you could get your legs broken. "We've got to talk about 'Good Morning, Brooklyn,'" he said ominously. He explained that Marisa Tomei didn't want to do the sketch, though he promised to try and talk her into it. I decided I would do the same.

I found her again by Marci's office and confronted her. "Why don't you want to do 'Good Morning, Brooklyn'?" I asked her straight out. She began rambling that after the movie *My Cousin Vinny*, she didn't want to be typecast as an Italian chick. She didn't want people to think that was all she could do. I told her that the sketch was great for her and it was funnier *because* she was in *My Cousin Vinny*. People wanted to see her do something like this, I pleaded. She wouldn't budge.

I knew that if I pressed her further I would run the risk of pissing the host off. I didn't think Marisa Tomei telling Lorne what an asshole I was would be a good way to get more airtime. You could try and change the host's mind, but if he or she didn't want to do your sketch, what could you do? Nothing. It was eliminated. For the rest of the week, with your legs broken, you would crawl in and out of studio 8-H and curse every sketch that was being rehearsed.

I never believed that everything happens for a reason. I have always known, however, that everything does happen. My campaign for the sketch to remain in the lineup was legitimate, and I was grateful to Downey for going to bat for me. But I hated Marisa Tomei. I didn't believe that she was worried about her public perception. I still don't. She didn't want to do the sketch the moment she found out that I wasn't a cast member. I wanted to choke her during Good-nights.

After the Marisa Tomei show, I was on camera in only bit parts for the next two weeks. That brought the grand total of sketches of mine that had gotten on the air in my second season to zero. Mohr: 0–4. Nothing had changed from my first year. I was still a bit player. I grew more and more nervous as the weeks ticked by. I could no longer place the blame on the fact that I was new.

But in the fifth week, I had a reversal of fortune. "Good Morning, Brooklyn" was back on the corkboard as the lead sketch, with Sarah Jessica Parker hosting. Suddenly I was walking on air. The sketch was slotted first, so it must have had universal approval. I figured that "Good Morning, Brooklyn" was my "Wayne's World," my "Church Lady," my "Hans and Franz." It was going to be the sketch that broke me.

Rehearsals went off without any glitches. The sketch was practically uncuttable. The host was getting big laughs, as were Farley, Sandler, and Janeane Garofalo. But during the Saturday afternoon rehearsals, a new storm began brewing. One of the producers pulled me aside and told me we had a big problem: A group called the Sons of Italy were going to protest the show if my sketch aired. The Sons of Italy apparently thought my sketch portrayed Italians in a negative light. It was further explained that unless I toned down some of the Eye-Tal-Yan jokes, the sketch would be yanked from the show.

I pleaded my case. The entire sketch was about Italians, and toning it down was the equivalent of making it less funny. A one-sided compromise was reached: I could probably keep the sketch on the air if I made it less Italian. Were they kidding me? How was I supposed to make a sketch about Italians less Italian? Mike Shoemaker asked me about the names of the two hosts: Did they have to be so stereotypical? Stereotypical? I had named the lead character after someone I knew. Go tell the Barone family in Verona, New Jersey, that they're too stereotypical! There was no way I was changing the name James Barone. Instead, I changed Angela Tucci to Angela Evans. My legs were fractured but not broken.

It was a move that bothers me to this day. In the original version, when we both said our names, the audience knew right away what we were doing. We were doing a sketch about Italians hosting a morning talk show. Now, with Sarah introducing herself as Angela Evans, the audience wasn't sure what they were about to watch.

The sketch remained atop the corkboard between dress rehearsal and air, but murmurs of protests from the Sons of Italy made their way to my ears. I remembered when Adam Sandler had done a Canteen Boy sketch that the Boy Scouts of America objected to.

A popular character of Adam's, the Canteen Boy was slow, if not slightly retarded. Whenever you wrote a character that was an audience favorite, the trick was to ride that character as long as possible. This particular week, Canteen Boy was going to take place at a Boy Scout camp (with cohost Alec Baldwin playing the troop leader). In the sketch, Alec would eventually wind up sharing a sleeping bag with Canteen Boy and begin fondling him. We all thought it was hysterical. The Boy Scouts of America did not.

JAY MOHR

After the "Boy Scouts Canteen Boy" sketch aired, the wall outside of Lorne's office where the letters to the show were posted was covered in letters of outrage. The most prominent letter had the Boys Scouts of America letterhead on it. The brass at Boy Scout headquarters were less than thrilled that a troop leader was portrayed as a pedophile. What made the situation worse was that the wardrobe department had outfitted those of us in the sketch in actual Boy Scout uniforms. They weren't replicas, and there was no possible substitute for Boy Scouts in the piece. We called ourselves Boy Scouts, we dressed as Boy Scouts, and Alec Baldwin played a Boy Scout leader who molested Canteen Boy. The Boy Scouts threatened the show with litigation, which I never understood. What was the show supposed to do? Take the sketch back? Turn back time and rewrite it? So periodically someone from outside would get a red ass about something that aired and write a letter telling us how much trouble we were all in, but eventually, more interesting letters would arrive and the protests would go into the trash can.

As airtime neared, I blocked out the threat of letters from the Sons of Italy papering the hallway outside Lorne's office and tried to focus on the sketch. It was a big break for me to have the first sketch of the night, and I didn't want to experience anything but satisfaction.

"Good Morning, Brooklyn" got huge laughs on the live show, but something was gnawing at me. In the wee hours of the morning, after the wrap party, I was home in my bed when I had a troubling thought. The "Canteen Boy" sketch was protested by the Boy Scouts *after* it aired. "Good Morning, Brooklyn" was being protested *before* it left the building. How could people object to a sketch if they hadn't seen it? It was just words on pieces of paper that went from my office to the read-through table to the eighth floor for rehearsal. Did the Sons of Italy have the writers' room bugged? Did they watch rehearsals? Or was it all a prank?

I still don't know, but when Courteney Cox hosted later that season, I brought back "Good Morning, Brooklyn." Again, it was the lead sketch. I obediently wrote "Angela Evans" into the sketch to avoid any pre-show controversy. I also resolved not to be pushed around by a dubious-sounding organization named the Sons of Italy—and to emerge with my legs intact.

As we were coming back from commercial break during the live show, I leaned over to Courteney Cox. "There's been a rewrite," I whispered. "No matter what it says on the cue card, make sure you say Angela Tucci, not Angela Evans." She introduced herself as Angela Tucci, and the audience burst out laughing.

The Sons of Italy didn't show up at the wrap party to take me for a drive into the weeds in Secaucus. I checked the wall for the next few weeks to see if there were any letters complaining about the sketch being too Italian. If there were, no one took the time to post them. For the rest of my time on the show, I was really bothered by the whole situation. However, after the sketch had worked twice, I decided that I no longer wanted to strangle Marisa Tomei.

After Sarah Jessica Parker hosted, I was on a bit of a roll. I brought back Christopher Walken with John Turturro— at his request. Turturro also did a Christopher Walken impression, and in the pitch meeting, he brought up that he wanted to do a Walken sketch. He said this in front of everyone, and it made me feel needed. I also played Harvey Keitel in the John Turturro show, so I had two fun impressions to do that week, and neither of them were cut.

In the Walken sketch, John Turturro played Christopher Walken's brother, Eugene. His impression was so funny that when he first spoke, I laughed directly into camera. The audience laughed when I laughed and I was never reprimanded for it. For one show, I was on fire, and I was having the greatest time of my life. Then they sent me back to the bench. In baseball, when you're hitting, you expect to stay in the lineup. Not on *Saturday Night Live.*

After John Turturro said his Good-nights, I had done three good sketches in two weeks; two of them I had written myself and one was the lead-off sketch. I anticipated that I would get more and better parts in read-through since I had shown what I could do in the last few shows. I didn't. If the sketch that I wrote myself didn't get picked to be on the show, my only shot of being on camera was if Tim Herlihy or Fred Wolf looked out for me. They always did, and in each show, I would have a few lines in someone else's sketch.

But after John Turturro left, I went five weeks straight with virtually no airtime. Nothing I wrote was picked to be on the show. Out of eleven shows that had come and gone in my second season, sketches that I had written were in only two of them. I started to fear for my job security. They had every right to fire me if they wanted to. I was freezing.

During my cold streak, I didn't mingle much with the other cast members. There was nothing to say. We didn't have anything in common. They were on television and I wasn't. Even when someone was being kind and offered words of encouragement, I felt empty. It never made me feel any better. I hated that I was in a situation where others felt they had to console me.

Because I wasn't on camera very often, I had plenty of free time on Saturday nights to roam around and meet the people who worked in the building. The undercover police officers who handled security for the show became good friends of mine. I got to know Jane, who worked as a janitor for the show, and I befriended Theresa, the NBC nurse. I spoke at length with all of them and found myself seeking their company each Saturday. They were beautiful, friendly people with families, pension plans, and summer homes. And like me, they were never on camera.

The undercover cops and I hit it off pretty quickly. They were blue-collar guys named Ron, Billy Mac, and Fat Phil. They dressed in suits and wore tiny earpieces to communicate with one another. They also carried .22-caliber pistols in their socks. I would chat with them during the show, and at the wrap party, they would always help me sneak in some extra friends. At the parties I would get so drunk that I couldn't walk anymore. I always made sure my drinking took place in their sights. If I finally snapped, I wanted to make sure I did it in front of the guys who were packing.

The NBC nurse, Theresa, was a delightful woman. She had a husband and a house somewhere in New Jersey, and she always had a smile on her face. I confided in her about my panic attacks and even showed her my Klonopin pocket. Having a nurse close by was always comforting. Since NBC gave free flu shots to its employees at the beginning of the cold and flu season, I felt relieved to be friends with the person who would be injecting me.

I didn't get a flu shot my first season and paid the price for it. I was flat out in my bed for a week with a fever. My second season, I decided to let NBC give me my flu shot. I couldn't afford to miss a minute of work, let alone a week. I was afraid that if I was ever sick in bed again, I might not get up to come back when I felt better.

But the day of the free NBC flu shots, Theresa wasn't there. She had taken a day off and there was a different nurse in her place. I wasn't too crazy about someone I had just met giving me a shot. What bothered me the most was that I had heard that after you get a flu shot, you contract flulike symptoms for a few days and, in some cases, even a fever. For some reason, this information terrified me. Still, I forced myself to go to the nurse's station the day they gave out the shots. I wondered if Theresa's absence should be taken as some sort of omen. I rolled up my sleeve and let the substitute nurse shoot me in the arm with the needle. It didn't hurt, and I suddenly felt manly and relieved. I proudly rolled down my sleeve when the substitute nurse shouted, "Oh my God! I am *so* sorry! You're not allergic to chicken feathers, are you?"

How the hell did I know if I was allergic to chicken feathers? Now I was certain that I was. The substitute nurse quickly downplayed the entire thing, but I could tell from her initial outburst that she had really messed up. I walked out of the NBC nurse's station planning the lawsuit that I would bring against NBC for shooting me with a needle full of chicken feathers. Henceforth, the show would be called *Jay Mohr's Saturday Night Live*.

The rest of the night I itched all over my body and felt nauseated. I was sure that any minute my windpipe would close up and I would choke to death. I never saw the substitute nurse after that night. I told Theresa the next time I saw her what had transpired. She was appalled that anyone would give another human being a flu shot without asking him if he was allergic to chicken feathers first. I was glad she was back.

Jane the janitor was probably the most refreshing person to talk to in the entire building. A black woman in her sixties, she didn't have an ounce of show business in her. Usually when I saw her, she was pushing a gigantic trash barrel on wheels. She always had a genuine smile on her face and seemed happy to see me. When we spoke, it was never about the show. It was always about family. During these conversations we were never interrupted. It was as if there was a shield around us.

During my spectator period, I would sit with the show's announcer, Don Pardo, who would sip tea to keep his throat loose and ask me about my parents. He also lived in New Jersey, and despite the generation gap, we knew many of the same places. He cracked me up. I had started talking with Pardo the moment I was hired on the show. When he first laid eyes on me in the hallway outside of studio 8-H, he shouted in the same voice he used for the show's introduction, "Ladies and gentlemen . . . *Jay Mooohr!*" He had been the voice of NBC for so many years and had done so many commercials that whenever he spoke to me, I felt comfortable. I had heard Don Pardo's voice so often that when he spoke, I felt as if I was sitting at home in my living room. Hearing Don

Pardo shout my name was a career wake-up call. I must have arrived if Pardo was saying my name.

Once I asked Don Pardo who was his all-time favorite out of all the musical guests that ever appeared on *Saturday Night Live*. He answered in his booming voice, "Are you kidding me, man? B.J." I asked him, "Billy Joel?" Pardo erupted, *"Bon Jovi!"* I was surprised, to say the least. Pardo was at least seventy years old, and his declaration caught me off balance. When I asked him if he was serious, he smiled. "That motherfucker can sing," he said. Fair enough. Maybe it was a Jersey thing.

Don Pardo, Theresa the nurse, Jane the janitor, and officers Ron, Billy Mac, and Fat Phil all helped make my Saturdays seem bearable. They listened to me and always had something nice to say. They never wanted anything from me but to see me smile. As I spent more and more time with them, it began to dawn on me that for whatever reason, these people simply liked me. Not me the performer or me the comic. They never saw that when they looked at me. They liked me for who I was. There wasn't a phony bone in any of them, and I loved them for it.

LORNE

THOUGH I had always heard wildly varied descriptions of Lorne Michaels, I really liked him. To hear fans of the show tell it, Lorne was the guy that changed television. Here was a guy who came out of nowhere—Toronto, actually—and made an indelible mark on the entertainment landscape with *Saturday Night Live*. He was immortal. He was a guy who told the network and the entire old establishment of America to stick it. He broke the biggest comedy stars ever, and he created a new kind of celebrity, a cool not-ready-for-prime-time-players celebrity. And it was all because of Lorne Michaels, genius.

But to some people in the entertainment community—and certainly many former cast members—Lorne

Michaels was downright diabolical. To them, Lorne was a man who would step on his grandmother's throat to make a nickel. He was daft and put on airs. He was completely out of touch, notably with how uncool he had become. He also had no recollection of how cool he once was. I always figured the real Lorne Michaels was somewhere between these two versions, and I never had any sense that he was operating on some sort of diabolical level.

Some past and present cast members were convinced that Lorne wouldn't sleep at night unless he made their lives miserable. Not me. No matter how pissed I ever got at Lorne Michaels, I never forgot what he had done for me. I had an illness that the show's lack of structure brought out of me. I had spent hours at a time on my knees praying to God not to let me die in my office or dressing room. I had suffered panic that I wouldn't wish on my worst enemy. But I was also occasionally on television, and when I was, it was on *Saturday Night Live*. I had legitimacy. I was making a fortune performing stand-up at colleges and clubs. People stopped me on the street and in the malls and shook my hand. I walked into auditions with credibility. I never forgot for a second that all of it was because at some point Lorne had nodded his head. At some point in the hiring process, out of the hundreds of people that auditioned for the show, Lorne Michaels said, "Him."

Whatever Lorne might have been, I do know he was

unflappable. The only story I heard about him breaking character happened when the band Skid Row was on the air. During the live show, Lorne always sat in a director's chair under the bleachers, and he always had an Amstel Light at the ready. The show was live and Skid Row was introduced. Sebastian Bach took the mike and said, "It's good to be here and we are live, motherfuckers!" Lorne dropped his Amstel Light onto the stage floor. Instantly he regained his composure, turned to one of the stage managers, calmly said, "Cancel their second song," and walked away.

I know enough to know how historically significant Lorne is to television. He definitely broke the back of the Lawrence Welk America. In my mind, he had started it all: antiestablishment, underground cool, late-night television. He created the mold and then threw it away. Every other imitator in his wake failed. *Saturday Night Live* originally went on the air in 1975, and Lorne Michaels has been executive producer of every episode, except for a brief hiatus from 1980 to 1985. How many people have produced the same television show for that long? Zero.

Even the supposed bombs of movies that Lorne produces are cash cows. They cost practically nothing to make, and they're already written by the time you get the idea to put them on film. In my opinion, the guy has written the book on how to be successful. Professionally speaking, if I were to analyze his career, I would have to give him As across the board. Personally speaking, I didn't really form a clear-cut opinion of Lorne. As the Brits might say, I always found him to be rather pleasant, but mind you, I rarely actually saw him.

I would joke to people who asked me how he was to work with that he was like Charlie on *Charlie's Angels*. I seldom laid eyes on him, but each week he was the one providing me with my mission. Oddly, I never heard him crack a joke either. Was he funny? He had delivered the great line "If you want to pay Ringo less, it's okay with me." So when friends would ask me what type of guy Lorne was, all I could muster was an "I don't really know."

Lorne's office was on the other end of the seventeenth floor from the writers' room, as well as from the offices of most of the cast and the writers. I'm sure this was by design. With the exception of waiting for the Monday-night pitch meeting to begin, there was never a reason for you to be hanging around his office. You could pretend that you were reading letters of protest for only so long.

Lorne had an incredible number of secretaries. Stories about the show say they are called the Lorne-ettes. When I was on the show, I never heard anyone ever refer to them that way. They were all called by their names. They were all pretty beautiful, too. That, I'm sure, was also by design. There were at least five, but probably more. I could never make a definite head count because they were never all at their desks at the same time. But they were certainly there. No one could walk unimpeded to Lorne's office without passing at least one of them. Checkpoint after checkpoint stripped you of your privacy as you arrived at the door.

One thing was clear about Lorne: He was the master of our domain. In a strange way, the show ran itself until he felt like running it. I just didn't know from where or when he did it. Though he did it rarely, Lorne made it clear he was the boss. During my second season when Lorne was addressing the outside rumors of the show's impending demise, he lectured us. "Many of you hear things from the outside about how the show is doing," he began. "I want to remind you that no one will ever stop you on the street to tell you how poorly you are doing. They will tell you only nice things, no matter how bad it's going. If you don't want to be here, there's the door, and that's the only thing keeping you from being a third lead on a sitcom."

Though he meant it as a jab, I remember counting seven people in the room who would be great third leads on sitcoms and wondering if they were thinking what I was thinking: That would be unbelievable. Alas, he was right. When I left *SNL*, I became the third lead on *The Jeff Foxworthy Show*.

Most of us saw Lorne only on Mondays during the pitch meeting with the host, on Wednesdays at the table read-through, and on Saturdays during the rehearsals and the taping of the show. Unless you had a prescheduled meeting with him, any encounter was purely coincidental. Lorne wasn't in the office as much as the rest of the *SNL* cast and crew, and when he was there, he was in seclusion. There weren't any announcements when he entered the building either. The only time he gave me direct advice was after "Psychic Friends Network" was cut from the Shannen Doherty show. I told him that I was going to resubmit the sketch in two weeks when John Malkovich hosted, and he advised me: "No, do it this week. You have guilt and momentum on your side."

My second season on the show, I had managed to schedule a one-on-one meeting with Lorne. It was more than halfway through the season, and I was so unhappy with my lack of screen time that I figured I was going to take my complaint right to the top. I had bitched and moaned for so long to so many people that it was my only remaining option.

I made a list of the shows I hadn't been on. The list also contained all the sketches I had written that I felt should have made it on the air but had fallen into the department of dead letters. I was taking the meeting with Lorne Michaels seriously. I couldn't have been more prepared. I had lists, for crying out loud.

At the appointed hour, I presented myself to one of his secretaries and she asked me to wait. So there I sat for the next half hour in front of his platoon of secretaries. None of them tried to engage me in any small talk.

They just kept answering their telephones and typing at their computers. I went over my lists. I knew that I was probably going to get only one shot. There was no one above Lorne. I was on my final appeal.

Eventually one of the secretaries told me I could go in, but that proved tougher than it should have been. The door was closed, and when I tried to push it open, it felt unusually heavy. As I was opening it, it caught on the carpet on Lorne's side. I had to either plow forward with the door or bend down and fold the carpet back down on the floor to get inside. Paranoid about knocking something over, I bent down, pulled the carpet out from under the door, and reassembled it so I could swing the door over it.

As I stood up after fixing the carpet, I saw Lorne sitting at his desk. He invited me in. I wasn't sure if I should close the door behind me or not. Since I had gone to all the trouble of figuring out the door's arc on the floor, I decided to close it. By the time I turned back around, Lorne had crossed to the front of his desk. The moment the door clicked shut, he put his hands in his pockets and told me that he wanted to apologize for the fact I had been used so infrequently. He went on to say how much I figured in the long-term plans of the show. "You are the future of the show," he said.

It was incredible. By the time it was my turn to speak, the only thing left for me to say was thank you. He had completely disarmed me. I never got to my lists. He took them away from me. He stripped me of every possible complaint. He covered everything that I was going to bring up and addressed it with assurance—though somehow I didn't feel particularly reassured.

Even though I was suffering from a serious drought of stage time, I never lost sight of the value of *Saturday Night Live* as a social chip. To be able to invite your friends to the live show was powerful. As they looked around, I could see in their eyes how cool a place it was. Being inside the machine for so long had caused me to lose sight of that. Regardless of this coolness, I still had to get away, so I flew to Los Angeles every break we had.

These breaks were either one or two weeks long, and I commuted with no fear of having a panic attack on the plane. When the breaks rolled around, I was too tired to panic. All I could do was sleep. Having my legs broken week after week consumed every ounce of energy that I had. Whenever it was time for me to go back to New York, Nicole and I would get into huge arguments. They were usually over nothing, and were fueled more by booze than any animosity.

Long after my career at *Saturday Night Live* was over, I realized why we were arguing so much then. It was because in my demented head, the arguments made her easier to leave behind. When I was in New York, I dreamed of being with her. I dreamed of being in Los Angeles with her and the sunshine. The women I saw in New York disgusted me. The same social chip that I could cash with my friends was the only thing I had to offer them. I hated them for that. I hated myself, too.

U2 has a song on their album *Achtung Baby!* called "Light My Way" that talks about a woman's love being a lightbulb hanging over your bed. My wife-to-be was my lightbulb. She lit my way. I believe that all human beings have a light inside of them. The light in me was getting very dim. I felt like a complete failure. Batting two for eleven in my second season was a disgrace.

By that point, when people asked me what I did for a living, I stopped telling them that I was on *Saturday Night Live* because I really wasn't. I would simply tell them that I was a comic. If I told someone I was on the show, they would always look excited at first and then eventually they would turn skeptical. They would ask me what characters I did, and if they hadn't seen the Christopher Walken sketch, I would have to name other sketches where I had stood in the background mimicking a prop. As far as being a celebrity goes, I didn't have anything to offer except stories about the people I worked with who were actually famous.

At least there were plenty of those.

When Roseanne hosted the show, she was famous. She was also out of her fucking mind.

I have always been a fan of the television show *Roseanne*, and I respected Roseanne as a comedian. Roseanne was pleasant to me and never did anything to me to distort my perception of her. I'd read the tabloid journalism about her, but I'd never paid any attention to it. When Roseanne arrived on the Monday of the week she was to be host, it was like meeting a bossy, wry old housewife. By Saturday, she was like a six-year-old.

The cast had filed into Lorne's office between dress rehearsal and air and taken up their positions. Some muttered to themselves about their sketches being dropped from the rundown. Lorne waited for everyone to settle and began to give notes. The moment he started to speak, Roseanne belched.

At first we thought it was by accident. Roseanne excused herself and motioned for Lorne to continue. As Lorne detailed the changes being made to the show, Roseanne continued to belch. She wasn't doing it by accident, either. She would belch to punctuate a particular note of Lorne's. She would belch during people's questions to Lorne. After each burp, she would look around the room and smile as if we were all in a grade school classroom. Her burps weren't exactly ladylike, either. She was letting out some real whoppers. Halfway through the meeting Roseanne literally ran out of gas.

Refusing to stop a good party, Roseanne started to make herself burp. If she opened her mouth to burp and nothing came out, she would hold up her hand and say, "Wait! Wait!"

Lorne wasn't waiting. During the entire meeting, he acted as if her antics weren't happening. There were a few scattered giggles at first when the belching began, but they quickly dissipated. Farley thought it was funny, so he threw out a couple of fake burps. As she continued the burping, it became unfunny fast and Farley stopped. Lorne spoke to us softly and made eye contact with everyone in the room. The more Roseanne burped, the quieter Lorne spoke. We had to lean in toward him to make sure we weren't missing anything. I wasn't on the show, so I had no reason to be attending the show meeting, but I was, and I was hanging on to Lorne's every word. Lorne's professionalism and savvy obliterated Roseanne's little-kid routine. It was impressive, to say the least. Because of Lorne's low voice, Roseanne's burps were just annoying.

A few minutes before the meeting ended, Roseanne gulped a bellyful of air and let out a monster. With a stern look, the assistant stage manager, Bob Van Rye, shushed her. The scoldings only made Roseanne's burps more important to her. When the meeting was over, she walked out of the office burping. My take on this is that she is obviously mentally ill.

Initially, the weird stuff that would happen in meetings with the hosts would incite panic attacks. But by the midpoint of the second season, these happenings simply amused me. On show number ten, I wasn't in any sketches, Luscious Jackson was the musical guest, and Jeff Daniels got his face ripped off.

The culprit was a prosthetic. When prosthetics are applied, the makeup department uses a special glue that cannot be taken off your face without first being loosened by an acetone solution. To remove the prosthetic, the makeup people would dip the edge of their paintbrushes in the solution, slice little lines through the prosthetic pieces, and then slide the brush up under the prosthetic to separate it from the skin. There was no other way to get it off.

But somehow, there was a mixup on the Friday night that Jeff Daniels had his life cast removed. The jar of solution labeled as prosthetic glue was in fact some kind of Krazy Glue. When the life cast was being taken off Jeff, the acetone solution wasn't working. The makeup artist tugged and pulled on the prosthetic and it became obvious that something was wrong. Someone had Krazy Glued the prosthetics onto Jeff Daniels's face!

I was later told that it was around midnight on Friday when Jeff finished rehearsals and the makeup department began removing his life cast. There weren't any doctors available at that hour, and taking the star of *Saturday Night Live* to the emergency room the night before his live performance wasn't a viable option. Someone at the show had the bright idea to call downtown to the New York University Medical School, and an hour later, four or five interns arrived at the eighth floor of 30 Rock and began the process of injecting Novocain through the life cast into Jeff Daniels's face.

After Daniels's face was numb, the interns ripped the prosthetic pieces off his face, taking off a layer of skin with it. The story was that Jeff was in so much pain that he ripped the arms off the makeup chair, a feat requiring near superhuman strength, as the chairs were built like old barbershop chairs.

It was quite a mystery as to how the mixup occurred. The makeup artist swore the jar was labeled correctly—meaning that someone had deliberately switched the safe glue with the Krazy Glue. The makeup artist who put the glue on was a guy named Jack, and he was always straight with me. Honest and professional, Jack was another lifer who had been with the show since the first episode. If he said the jar was labeled correctly, then it was labeled correctly. In fact, the other makeup artists were kind and honest, too, and I couldn't imagine any of them pulling such a nasty stunt. But someone was hiding the truth, and to the best of my knowledge, nobody ever figured out what really happened.

Jeff Daniels, however, was the ultimate pro. He returned on Saturday night and did the show. I couldn't detect any layers of skin missing from his face.

When George Foreman hosted, he didn't bring his grill, but he did talk to me about real fear. That week I had a bit part in a "Motivational Speaker" sketch with him about a guy who lived in a van by a riverbed, but it started nowhere and went nowhere. It wasn't Foreman's fault. With athletes, it was a roll of the dice because they aren't actors. When athletes are on the show, it isn't a fish-out-of-water situation; it is more like a fish from another planet. The booking of an athlete was always a big coup—Joe Montana after he wins the MVP award in the Super Bowl or Wayne Gretzky after he breaks the all-time scoring record—but historically, the shows with athletes are the least funny. I didn't really care if Foreman could be funny, because all I wanted to talk to him about was boxing. How often do you meet someone who fought both Ali and Frazier?

I called Foreman "Champ"—which is a word people throw out all the time—because he really was. I asked him what his mindset was when he crawled through the ropes. "I'm scared," he told me, "because that other guy across the ring trained his whole life to punch me in the face, and people get hurt in my business." This was not what I expected to hear out of the mouth of the man who beat Joe Frazier like a redheaded stepchild.

While there was always some fear lurking in me, being on the show was hardly the same as entering the ring in a heavyweight title fight. I had overcome my anxiety about the lack of a take two, and I just wanted to show everyone what I could do. My feeling now was "Put me in, Coach," and once I was in, it was "Please hit the ball to me." There was no real fear of failure or success— just the fear of not getting to the plate.

Courtney Love's band, Hole, was the musical guest the week that Foreman hosted, and she brought Frances Bean, her baby with Kurt Cobain, along with her. At first

JAY MOHR

I was appalled at the number of nannies—male and female—doting on this baby. Then I realized something strange. They weren't really nannies; they were guys from the neighborhood. They could've even been roadies. They didn't look like they had had any formal nanny training or were even particularly good with kids. Halfway through the show, another thought hit me: It was past midnight and the baby was awake. Why wasn't she in the hotel asleep? Because she was being passed around among these rocker maggot types while her mommy rocked the place.

TLC was even more ridiculous. They arrived with an entourage of at least forty people. It was as if there was someone to work the pinky, someone else to move the index finger, and another person to watch over the thumb. The band members all wore overalls with sweatshirts tied around their waists. After each rehearsal, a guy who probably made $50,000 a year would walk out onstage and adjust the knot in each of their sweatshirts. That was all he did. A different person measured the distance between the girls' wrists and the cuffs on their sweatshirts. There was something silly about the whole TLC thing, like Lisa "Left Eye" Lopez's not being recognizable without wearing a pair of eyeglasses with a condom in the left eye and the name of their hit, "Don't Go Chasing Waterfalls."

I was going to do my best not to go chasing any waterfalls in Manhattan.

———

Even when things were going my way, there was always a hitch. I had done Christopher Walken twice my first season on the show. My second season, people would stop me on the street and ask me when I was going to do more Walken. I didn't want to do the same sketch over and over, so I tried working with a few of the writers to come up with something really different.

When I returned for my second season, I had come back with three other killer impressions to add to Walken: James Woods, Rush Limbaugh, and Phil Gramm, the U.S. senator from Texas who was then running for president. But Jim Downey told me that I was too young to play Phil Gramm, and no one was interested in my doing Woods. When a Limbaugh sketch hit the read-through table, I pleaded my case, volunteering to put on full makeup and a prosthetic and audition, but I was waved off. Instead, Farley was pegged to do Limbaugh and it didn't work, which was too bad. Even though Farley had a free lifetime pass as far as I was concerned, it was sad to watch him do something that was not funny.

As I focused on revisiting Walken, most of the ideas people had were funny but not funny enough to be on the show until Steve Lookner approached me one Tuesday night with an idea that I knew would make the cut. Lookner was one of the Harvard guys that Dave Attell and I had run out of the office, and I didn't see much of him anymore, since guys stayed with the writing groups where they felt most comfortable. My group consisted mainly of me. I was staring at the walls waiting for something to enter my brain when Lookner stuck his head in the doorway and asked to show me something, which turned out to be a finished sketch of Christopher Walken doing a commercial for Skittles. It was certainly different, and it was definitely hilarious.

However, the Skittles sketch had a few things going against it. First and foremost, I was the only one in the sketch. Further down the list, the host wasn't in it and neither were any of the women. I felt in my gut that there was no way a solo sketch with just me in it would make its way onto air, but Lookner and I stayed up until five in the morning rewriting it, and we submitted it for read-through.

At the table read on Wednesday, Lookner and I were both excited. Even if the sketch wasn't picked to be on the air, it was going to be a lot of fun reading it in front of everybody. "Skittles" got many more laughs than I had anticipated at the read-through, and Lookner and I waited around afterward to see if it would be picked.

When the door to Lorne's office swung open, we were afraid to go in and look. We felt that if it was picked, we would have pulled off a coup of sorts. We took our time walking down the hallway toward the corkboard, giggling nervously the whole way. By the time we made it to Lorne's, people were already filing out. Some looked pissed off, some looked happy. As we made our way closer and closer, a few people passed us and offered congratulations.

They had to be pulling our legs, right? When Fred Wolf walked by and offered his congratulations, we knew we had done it. Fred was the type of guy who would never lie about a sketch being picked for air. By the time Lookner and I reached the inside of Lorne's office, no one else was there. We just stood alone staring at the corkboard. Thumbtacked at the bottom was a blue index card that read "Skittles." We high-fived each other, and I came darn close to hugging him. With two versions of "Good Morning, Brooklyn" under my belt and now Walken doing a Skittles commercial, I really felt like I was finally showing my stuff.

The sketch went well at dress rehearsal, but not so great that it was uncuttable. After dress rehearsal, not only was "Skittles" still in the lineup, but a few sketches ahead of it were cut, so I had actually moved up in the show. I was ecstatic. I tried not to smile while Lorne gave us all notes. The last thing someone whose sketch just got cut wanted to see was me gloating from across the room.

As was customary, the sketch had been timed during dress rehearsal. (All sketches were timed so the show would fill ninety minutes, and the time allotted the sketch was written on the index card under the title.) Under the word *Skittles* was the notation ":50." Who knew I could be so happy with less than sixty seconds of airtime? But happy I was.

Christopher Walken pitching Skittles was the only sketch I was in that week, but I was thrilled. It was strange enough and funny enough to inspire some watercooler conversations when people went to work on Monday.

I took my place on the stage, which was a basic green backdrop. There were no props other than a bag of Skittles that I would hold up halfway through the sketch. I stood there during commercial break, ready to rock and roll. We came back from the commercial break, the lights went up, and I started my impression. I looked into the camera and said, as Walken, "I would like to talk to you for a moment . . . about . . . Skittles."

The audience went batshit. They laughed much harder then they had during dress rehearsal. I was in heaven. The crux of a Christopher Walken impression is the awkward pauses in his speech pattern. Each time I took a pause, the audience would begin laughing and I would actually have to wait them out to say my line. It couldn't have been going any better. The sketch ended and the studio filled with applause. I floated off the stage as the studio went dark and the show went to commercial.

As I was walking from the stage to my dressing room, I saw Lorne walking toward me with an Amstel Light in his hand. I couldn't believe my good fortune. Finally I was going to get some love from the big man. As we were about five feet from each other, I slowed a bit, and sure enough, Lorne waved his hand for me to lean close to him. "That was a fucking minute and twenty seconds!" he said. And then he walked away.

I was crushed. I had just done one of the stranger and funnier sketches of the year, and here Lorne was tearing me a new asshole for going over fifty seconds. I wanted to turn to him and say, "Hey, sorry, they laughed so hard that they fucked up the time!" I was on Lorne's shit list for a week because of thirty seconds. My bad.

WEEKEND UPDATE

I NEVER THOUGHT that there was a conspiracy at *Saturday Night Live* to keep me off camera, nor do I believe that I was being forced to pay my dues. I can't recall anyone who has ever been hired on the show who immediately ate up major airtime. I do think, however, that the general belief on the show is that if you are new, the unspoken rule is that you are to be broken into the rotation gradually. But I felt like John F. Kennedy when he ran for the U.S. Senate: I refused to wait my turn.

I didn't see any benefit in waiting, either. I was a performer, and the show needed performances. Jim Downey once told me that the show goes through stages when it is performance-based and others when it is writer-based, and that when it goes through the writer-based stage, it suffers. When Billy Crystal, Martin Short, and Christopher Guest were on, it was amazingly funny because they were allowed to do whatever they wanted. How do you pitch Billy Crystal doing "You look maaa-velous!" at a table read? When I was there, Ed Grimley would never have gotten on the air because it would have had to be written, formatted, and put on the table for read-through on Wednesday, at which time Martin Short would've had to stand up on the table in front of a roomful of people and dance around. When I got there, they hired around sixteen new writers. It was like ROTC guys from the Harvard newsroom coming into Vietnam telling you which hill to take.

I had spent my whole life taking the stage and making people laugh. Sometimes I'd take a nap, wake up, and go onstage fifteen minutes later—and make people laugh. Other times I'd get high or drunk and go onstage—and make people laugh. Whether I was working a black room, a gay and lesbian club, or a college auditorium, there was always one constant: I would go onstage and make people laugh. I never understood why *Saturday Night Live* should be any different. After all, why hire a guy like me if you don't want a guy like me?

Of the cast members who were on the show during my stay, all of them were seldom used when they first arrived. Whether it was Mike Myers, Adam Sandler, or David Spade, they all spent more than a year or two saying one or two lines a week, if any. The fastest way to break this waiting period is to create an original character so funny that it's in the show's best interest to continue to put the character on air. Spade's was the Receptionist, Rob Schneider had Copy Guy, and Sandler's were Opera Man and Canteen Boy. The NBC gift shop located in the 30 Rock lobby sells coffee mugs and T-shirts with the most famous recurring *SNL* characters on them. I used to browse through the gift shop knowing I had a 20 percent NBC discount and dreaming of the day I could use it for merchandise bearing the imprint of one of my own original characters. I would look at the paperweights and greeting cards with my coworkers' faces on them and become insanely jealous.

Still, I never harbored any real animosity toward the show or any of the people who were in positions of power while I was on it. I always knew that the key to my success lay within me. Coming up with an idea to pitch to the host was difficult. Coming up with an original character to launch my *Saturday Night Live* career was maddening. I didn't want to have to wait my turn. I wasn't happy having one line in someone else's sketch. In hindsight, I was probably on the same path as everyone else who had ever been on the show. But *eventually* becoming a star wasn't what I had signed up for.

I did know that the easiest way for stand-up comics who are on *SNL* to get on the air is to do a feature during Weekend Update. When your well of ideas has run dry and there isn't an original character in your head, you could always write down some of your stand-up and submit it for Weekend Update. Chris Rock did this a lot, as did Spade when he started out. I was never comfortable with this process because I figured if my stand-up made Weekend Update, then I wouldn't be able to use it anymore in the comedy clubs. It was hard enough to come up with sketches twenty weeks of the year, but when those twenty weeks were up, I didn't want to have to write a new act as well.

I envisioned myself onstage someplace doing my routines with the audience staring blankly at me because they had already heard what I was telling them. So what I did was to devour all the newspapers I could get my hands on to find some current events items that I could write an Update piece on. Few of the pieces I wrote for Update were ever picked, but I was convinced that it had nothing to do with their humor content.

Sometimes I would write a Weekend Update piece that would get a lot of laughs at read-through or even rehearsal, but wouldn't be selected for the show. One sketch I wrote was about a guy who talks about how tricky investing in the stock market is, so he turns to currency trading. He goes to the airport and puts down a hundred bucks and receives several million pesos. "Now, I can't speak for everyone and I can't guarantee this investment will pay off, but I walked out of the airport with a few million bones in my pocket," he tells the audience. "I was on a hot streak until I put it all in German marks and lost half my money. So if you go to the airport, stick with the pesos."

"Lance Currothers" was an Update piece that *killed* at dress rehearsal but was killed before the live show. The sketch featured me as an obviously gay movie critic who sang his reviews. To the tune of Bruce Springsteen's "I'm on Fire," Lance sang: "Hey, little girl, is your daddy home? Or did he go and dress up like a woman from an old folks' home. Hey . . . he's a maid for hire. Go see *Mrs. Doubtfire.*" Lance would then score the movie on his Yaah-meter and let out a "yaahh." Though no one ever gave me a definitive reason, I knew that Jim Downey didn't like gay sketches, so I suspect his phobia did Lance in.

I had always thought that getting sketches on the air would be like playing baseball. If you're playing well and knocking the ball out of the park, you play. That wasn't the case for me. Some weeks I would write and act in the first sketch of the show. It would do great and I would think to myself, Great, now I'm on a roll! Then the wheels would just stop turning.

Often a sketch would be put on the air because certain performers in the sketch were light that week. Translation: They weren't on last week's show, and to pacify egos, the producers needed to put something with them in it on the air. How can the funniest sketches get on the air each week when the writers have that handicap? You stay up all night busting your ass and your sketch gets huge laughs at read-through, but the cork-board is loaded with sketches that are not as funny and are loaded with light cast members.

My second season on the show, I started to notice Lorne politicking a bit here and there. I would overhear him say things to Jim Downey like "Mike is light this week." I always thought it was a magnanimous gesture on his part, but I couldn't seem to get him to say it about me. This wouldn't have bothered me if better sketches were getting on, but they weren't. It would be reasonable to assume that the best sketches are the ones that make it on the air. Definitely not. If the women were light that week and there was a mildly amusing sketch that had all of them in it, that sketch was certain to be picked—though this wasn't only in regard to the women.

During my second season, Janeane Garofalo was hired midseason, presumably both to pump some life into *SNL* and to create sketches for the women. Though Janeane's very funny and a talented actress, she was a drag when she worked at *SNL*. Upon her arrival, Janeane told the press that the show was biased against women. What better way to motivate writers to write for you than to tell the *New York Post* that they don't want to write for you! She described the show as a boys' club and a frat house—though apparently no one was notified that I was a boy.

Janeane's comments were piling on. The reviews of

the show from my first season through the midpoint of the second ranged from savage to brutal. Critics called the show nothing short of humiliating, and headlines like "Saturday Night Dead" were commonplace in the New York tabloids. The negative reviews were almost always accompanied by a reference to the show's problem with women, which always burned my ass. Every so often Lorne would begin a pitch meeting by reassuring us that he knew we were working hard, but he certainly never would have addressed such an issue as one cast member complaining to the press about the show.

Aside from a few brief snickers behind closed doors, the Janeane matter was never openly addressed by the staff. Janeane and I were always friendly, and I'd often go down to Lundy's Deli with her and Chris Elliott for sandwiches and beers. However, I was annoyed at her for spouting off in public because I was one of those so-called oppressive white guys, and no one was writing for me, either. Many performers write their own sketches. That's one of the few ways you can attempt to control your destiny. Trust me, if Janeane wrote a funny sketch, it stood a great chance of being on the air because the writers were constantly being asked to create more sketches for the women on the show. The problem was, Janeane realized early on that she didn't want to be on *SNL*, so she didn't contribute anything.

Interestingly, when Jan Hooks and Nora Dunn were on the show, there were never any articles about the show hating women. The reason was elementary: Jan and Nora were two incredibly talented women who wrote their own sketches. I cannot remember a *Saturday Night Live* episode during the time they were in the cast that they weren't on the show. They produced, and they were given airtime because they were brilliant.

Perhaps Janeane's complaint should have been about the lack of female *writers* on the show. Nobody could argue with that. Out of twenty-two writers, only three were women. The female cast member ratio was only slightly better. My first season, the female cast members were Ellen Cleghorne, Melanie Hutsell, Julia Sweeney, and Sarah Silverman. My second season, Sarah left and Laura Kightlinger, Morwenna Banks, and Molly Shannon were added (along with Janeane in midseason). Out of this group, perhaps because she was new, Sarah Silverman wrote the most. Julia, who was a real sweetheart, kept bringing back her androgynous Pat, but while it was great in its time, there was no longer anything the least bit funny about it.

Though I didn't feel personally betrayed by Janeane because I wasn't the direct target of her complaints, I did work at *SNL*, and her bitching certainly wasn't helping the value of the property on which I wanted to build my dream house.

For some reason, Weekend Update pieces aren't chosen on Wednesday night with the rest of the show. In most

JAY MOHR

cases, it wasn't until Saturday afternoon when you learned the fate of your Update piece. When the rehearsal schedule was printed up on Wednesday night, all of the Weekend Update pieces submitted would be listed in the margin with the performers' initials printed next to them. Shortly before dress rehearsal on Saturday, one of the producers would approach you and tell you your piece was going to be rehearsed.

After you were given this news, the piece would quickly be written out onto cue cards. You were never told in advance exactly when during Weekend Update your piece would be performed. If more than one piece was submitted, you would be told the order in which they were being done, but that was it. You would have to stand off to the side of the Update desk as Norm Macdonald or Kevin Nealon read the news. Suddenly, Bob Van Rye, the stage manager, would whisper "Go," and you would slide into the chair next to the news anchor as quietly as possible. If none of the Update pieces at read-through were picked to be on the show, Adam Sandler was usually asked to come up with a song in ten minutes, and that was what they would go with.

The key to a Weekend Update piece, I learned, was that it had to be from the news. I remember Sarah Silverman doing an Update piece about her sister's wedding and Rob Schneider being furious that it was picked. When I defended the piece as funny, Schneider shot back: "It's not fucking news! It's the Weekend Update desk. A Weekend Update piece should be news."

I wrote a great Update piece that I never submitted my first season. It was a travel piece about England, and it went like this: "Hi, I just got back from England and they are still mad at us because they lost the Revolutionary War. Who could blame them? There were only nine of us. But hey, it's not our fault that they fought in the white snow wearing bright red uniforms. They were always standing in a straight line, too. Is that fair? They would charge with drums and flute while our guys sat behind rocks looking at each other and saying, 'I think I hear someone coming.'" It was written the week of the Jeff Goldblum show, and because my idea of his playing a dog had bombed, I chickened out.

I did get to do a "Dick Vitale: March Madness" Update piece. Originally it was written as an eight-page sketch by Steve Lookner. I read it at read-through. Halfway through it, I was out of breath from screaming. On page 6, I actually stopped reading, put the pages down, and reached for a bottle of water. I continued, and by the end I was ready to pass out. People around the table broke out into a sort of golf clap. A few were laughing and giggling. I didn't know if they thought it was funny or were just impressed I got through it all. Turns out, it was both.

The piece was edited down to a page and a half and submitted for Weekend Update. In it, I dressed up as Dick Vitale and mixed up my Oscar predictions with the NCAA basketball tournament. "Toughest region . . . best actress," I began, spraying my words à la Vitale. "No doubt about it, baby, number one seed is Holly Hunter in *The Piano*. Let's see her in action." Over a clip of Hunter in *The Piano,* I continued: "Look at her act. She's silent but deadly. She ain't talkin' for no one. She's just playin' the piano." I did each of the main categories, picking Ralph Fiennes in *Schindler's List* for best supporting actor because "he does it all—he shoots, he rebounds, he's a Nazi."

My second season, I wrote what was undeniably the funniest Update piece I had in me. At the time, the gubernatorial race was heating up in New York. The race was getting an incredible amount of press because Howard Stern had announced that he was going to run. Howard was way ahead of his time. We know now with the election of Jesse Ventura and the like how fed up voters had become with the standard bipartisan bullshit. Preliminary polls had Howard Stern pulling up to 30 percent of the vote, and it was beginning to look like he had an outside shot at actually becoming governor. New York State law requires all candidates to release full, comprehensive records of their incomes and properties. Calling this requirement ridiculous and in no way, shape, or form relevant to an election, Howard pulled out of the race. There was now no third-party candidate running for the office. That was when I stepped in.

I wrote my Weekend Update piece. My sketch was my announcement that I, Jay Mohr, was throwing my hat into the political ring and running for governor of the great state of New York. In the piece I admitted to know-ing next to nothing about politics or even the state of New York's needs or problems. My only platform was that I thought it would be a cool gig, and that if you voted for me, I would get you laid. That was it. Vote for me for governor and I will see to it that you get laid. I explained that I knew that there were a lot of ugly voters out there who weren't being accounted for. I went on to explain that I knew a lot of hot chicks, and because I worked in television, I could afford a lot of prostitutes.

I also told the voters that I knew they were probably wondering how a twenty-four-year-old New Jersey native could legally become governor of New York. I conceded that inasmuch as these were valid points, the people who enforce such election rules want to get laid, too. I told the voters that if I was elected, they could be assured that crime would be at an all-time low. Who wants to go out and commit crime when you could be staying inside get-ting laid? I confessed that in four years, when my term was up, the city would be a mess. The streets wouldn't be paved, taxes would be out of control, and nothing would've been accomplished. But no one would care— and we all know why. I finished the segment by saying: "So when you go to the voter's booth, know one thing, 'If I vote for Jay Mohr, I'm going to get laid.' See you at the polls!"

The piece made it to dress rehearsal, where it played well. All day Saturday I never once worried about whether my piece would get on. It had to. It had killed at the table

JAY MOHR

read, and people were coming up to me and talking about it in the hallways on Thursday and Friday. Not once on Saturday did I look in the margin of the show rundown to see what my competition was. I couldn't be denied this time.

Shortly before the live dress rehearsal the supervisor for Weekend Update, Herb Sargent, said he needed to see me. Seventy years old, Herb had thick white hair and big glasses. He looked as if he should have been on CNN hosting *Crossfire*. I still don't know what it is exactly Herb did for a living, though that was due mostly to the autonomy of Weekend Update. Herb told me that we had a problem. My Update piece couldn't be on the show. I was stunned. When I asked for a reason, he told me that the NBC censors had come down hard on him because of the content of the piece. I asked him to elaborate, and he said that you couldn't say *get laid* on television.

I stood there with my mouth hanging open and asked him if he was joking. He assured me that he wasn't. He repeated that *get laid* was never going to get past the censors, so the piece had to be pulled from the rundown. I was livid.

"Isn't this the same show that twenty-four years ago Chevy Chase called Richard Pryor a nigger?" I asked.

"I don't see what that has to do with this," he replied.

"It has a lot to do with this!" I interjected. "You want me to believe that you can say *nigger* on *Saturday Night Live*, but a quarter of a century later you can't say *get laid!*"

My anger didn't exactly make him want to circle the wagons for me, and I had a feeling that the censors and Herb had never even spoken to each other about my sketch. To this day, I don't believe you can't say *get laid* on television—especially since I've probably heard it said more than a hundred times since.

I had put all my eggs in one basket that week and had not written anything else. If I wasn't going to be on Update, I wasn't going to be on the show again. For the first time in weeks, I went back to my dressing room and just sat there. I sat there during the live rehearsal and I sat there during the show. I sat there during Good-nights, too. I didn't scribble on the walls or put my feet up against the door. I just stayed still and wondered long and hard why I had ever been hired.

Nicole came from Los Angeles to visit me in the middle of my second season. It was a relief for me to have some-one close to me witnessing everything I was. I could tell by the way she reacted and behaved that she was seeing many of the things I had told her about.

As her visit preceded a break, I flew back to Los Angeles with her. On the flight, we didn't talk about the show at all. When I left the building, I could no longer speak of the show. No matter who asked me about it or when, my descriptions of the show would deteriorate into a series of whines and groans. I was a great complainer. Even when I mentally reminded myself to act polite, I would soon be bitching and moaning. The people I complained to were either amazed or annoyed. There was seldom a middle ground.

The show was fascinating to everyone I spoke to. When I went on the road to do stand-up, I saw firsthand how diverse the show's audience was. I would be at a college talking with students and they would tell me who their favorite cast member was. In one town, audience members would tell me they loved Sandler, but in the next town over, they would tell me they hated him. These weren't shrug-of-the-shoulder types of discussions either. Everyone was overly passionate when they spoke with me about *Saturday Night Live*. They would fall all over themselves to tell me how much they loved the show, and I wouldn't know what to say next. I felt like a phony.

Nicole and I were about an hour into the flight when I had finished reading the sports page of the *New York Post*. I leafed through the rest of the paper and saw something about the show in the Page Six gossip column. In bold type I saw SATURDAY NIGHT LIVE and I stopped to read the item. The gossip column reported that Tom Arnold had had his birthday party the night before at the strip club Scores. The item detailed how Tom had partied well into the evening with his pals, *Saturday Night Live* stars Adam Sandler, David Spade, Tim Meadows, Chris Farley, and "Jay Moore." My name was broken up in the margin of the piece so the *Jay* was at the end of one line and the *Moore* was at the beginning of the line beneath it.

I turned to Nicole and showed her that my name was misspelled in the *New York Post*. She read the item and looked at me curiously. "You were with me last night," she said. She was right. I was with her the entire night, and was never near Tom Arnold or his birthday party at the strip club. I could tell that the false sighting bothered her, but my name being misspelled bothered me more than the false sighting. I laughed to myself. I was getting free publicity that wasn't true, and my name had been spelled wrong.

SIXTEEN

GIVE ME LITTLE BITS
OF MORE THAN I CAN TAKE

RICKI LAKE ended my drought. It
was the twelfth show of the season, and Tim Herlihy had
done more than look out for me. He sat down in his office
and stayed up all night writing with me. This was the first
time one of the writers had actually sought me out, sat
me down, and declared that we weren't leaving the room
until we finished the sketch. When Tim's phone rang, he
would answer it and tell the person on the other line that
he was busy and hang up. When someone walked into
his office, he brushed them off with a "not now."

In the sketch, I played Ricki Lake. I dressed in drag
and wore thick lipstick. Bob Newhart played a couples
counselor, and as Ricki Lake, I had him give advice to all
the freaks in the sketch. Being on the same stage as Bob

Newhart was surreal. I had spent every Monday night in high school watching *Newhart* on CBS. My parents and I never missed an episode. After I started doing stand-up comedy, I bought *The Buttoned Down Mind of Bob Newhart* and memorized it. The Ricki Lake sketch got good laughs, and I felt like it had a chance of being on the air again. I wanted to hug Bob Newhart for not telling me that he was being typecast and cutting it.

The week after Bob Newhart, Deion Sanders hosted and I was shut out again. What I had at read-through wasn't funny, and I knew it when I handed it in. I had two lines in a three-card-monte sketch. At this point, when I had only a few lines, I would rather have not been on the show at all. I was going to ask out of the three-card-monte sketch, but on Thursday I was added to another sketch. Since that sketch had Farley in it, I didn't care how many lines I had. I was there.

It was a hilarious sketch about commandos going into a spaceship that had landed. Each time some of the commandos would charge into the spaceship, they would reemerge with their clothes ripped off and tell the commander they had been raped. Deion was the commander, and he told us to keep charging in. When Spade came out of the UFO, he had the word *bitch* written across his chest in lipstick. It was great.

Eventually it was Farley's turn to storm the spaceship. Chris looked at Deion, cocked his assault rifle, and said he was going to go in there to kick ass and take names. Chris barreled up the stairs into the spaceship.

As he bent his head down to enter, his pants fell down, leaving his entire ass bare on live television. When Chris reached around to pull up his pants he was laughing and bumped his head on the doorway of the spaceship. He screamed out, "Son of A!" and wrestled with his pants.

It didn't matter what happened next—the show was over. Even during the last sketch of the night, the audience was still giggling and murmuring about the commando sketch. Farley had done it again. He had taken an ordinary show and turned it into watercooler conversation. I still wonder if his pants fell off by accident.

Moments like Chris's pants falling down made the show the greatest job that ever existed. As down as I got, I was sometimes picked up by the sheer magic of what happened around me. When Tom Petty performed, he brought Dave Grohl to be his drummer. Grohl recognized me from when Nirvana was on and said hello to me. When I asked him how it felt playing drums "for one of the old-timers," Grohl's eyes grew big as saucers, and he replied, "Dude, it is an honor." Petty rocked the place, singing "You Don't Know How It Feels to Be Me," and the musical message addressed my mood.

I was sure I wasn't imagining things when the band Live came through and performed a fantastic version of "I Alone." David Hyde Pierce hosted that show and it was one of the funnier ones of the season. At the after-party, everyone was feeling really good about everything and was chatting and drinking when something amazing happened. Live walked into the restaurant and everyone stopped what they were doing and greeted the group with a standing ovation. It was the only time during my two years that this ever happened. They deserved it. I, on the other hand, was feeling fortunate even to be invited to the after-parties. I was doing nothing again, and the thought of having another drought scared the shit out of me.

After "Ricki Lake" aired, I sat out the next two shows. I forced myself to write. I became a terrible human being. The more I tried to write, the more of an asshole I became. I argued with everybody. I asked people flat out if they would add me to their sketch. I begged. I also did something that I never thought I would ever do. I did something I still feel sick about.

I stole.

Paul Reiser hosted the fifteenth show of the season. He gave me a Cuban cigar and I chomped on it during our Greek restaurant sketch. I had only a few lines, but I figured that I should look the part. I sat on a stool behind the register looking rather belligerent and chomped and swallowed and chomped and swallowed, intermittently looking up at Paul and saying no. In the next sketch, a commercial for mouthwash, I was an extra in the boardroom and I felt like I was peaking on acid from the cigar.

The executives at the mouthwash company were trying to show the clients how clean and fresh it was. In the middle of the sketch, Tim Meadows knocks on the door and begins making out with Molly Shannon. The sight of a black guy and a white woman going at it is supposed to shock everyone. I sat there the entire time in a near state of panic, scanning the cue cards for my line. Every character's lines were in a different color on the cue cards. Chris Elliott's lines were green, Paul's were brown, and for the life of me, I couldn't remember what color I was. It wasn't until the band began to play that it dawned on me that I had no lines.

That was also the week I took Rick Shapiro's act and wrote it down word for word and submitted it as my sketch. Rick Shapiro was a comic in Greenwich Village. In his act, he did an impression of an Irish bartender who shouted at his customers. The skit was hilarious, and long before I got on *Saturday Night Live*, my friends and I had quoted it to one another. In the routine, a customer would approach the bar and inform the bartender that his drink order was wrong. The bartender would be polite and say, "Aw, I'm awfully sorry." He would continue: "Here's another drink you'll love. It's called, 'Get out! You're fired!'" Another patron in the routine would tell the bartender a joke and the bartender would say: "Aw, that's a great joke! You like jokes, do ya? Here's one for ya . . . Get out! You're fired!"

When the sketch was picked to be on the air, I was officially fucked. Rick Shapiro's Irish bartender sketch sailed through the Wednesday selection meeting and coasted smoothly through rehearsals on Thursday and Friday. It cleared the dress rehearsal on Saturday and wasn't cut after the live dress rehearsal that night. The show that had been selected in Lorne's office between dress rehearsal and air ran as scheduled, and the Irish bartender sketch was broadcast live across America. For a few weeks after the show aired, I avoided going to the comedy clubs for fear of bumping into Rick or any comic who had ever seen him perform, which was all of them.

Three weeks later, on Saturday night during the live dress rehearsal (the night that Courteney Cox hosted and I did my second "Good Morning, Brooklyn"), the show's supervising producer, Ken Aymong, called me over. I was on my way to the stage dressed as James Barone when he asked me to follow him. He led me to a room behind the control room that I had never been in before. In the room was a table with a few chairs and a small cabinet. On top of the cabinet was a television and a VCR. Sitting in front of the television was Lorne Michaels.

Ken asked me if I knew a guy named Rick Shapiro. I told him I did not. Ken then pressed play on the VCR, and in front of me on the monitor was a video of Rick Shapiro doing his act. On the tape in the VCR, he was doing the Irish bartender sketch. He was doing it exactly the way I copied it. Ken let the tape play a while. Finally Lorne asked me, "You've never heard of this guy or seen his act?" I replied that I had not. Lorne nodded his head and Ken Aymong turned off the VCR. Lorne looked at me for a second and said, "Okay." And I walked out of the room.

Later, I found out that Rick and his manager were suing the show. Why wouldn't they? I don't know the particulars but a settlement was reached, and in the settlement the Irish bartender sketch was edited out of all of the reruns. Undoubtedly I should have been fired, but I wasn't. I never saw Rick Shapiro again, but if I did, I would have acted as if I didn't see him. What I did was inexcusable, and no apology in the world could ever make up for it.

Whenever someone would ask me about the sketch and point out that it was in Rick's act, I would tell them that five different people had written the sketch and I was just put in it. Nobody bought it, and the reputation for being a thief followed me for quite a while in the only place I had ever felt comfortable: the comedy clubs.

After I stole Rick Shapiro's act, I didn't even know if I should bother handing anything in. Would Lorne believe I wrote it? I resubmitted a "Ricki Lake" sketch that had been cut earlier in the season and it didn't get on.

The week after Paul Reiser hosted, John Goodman and Dan Aykroyd cohosted and Bill Murray was floating through the hallways on Saturday, too. It was an exciting week for all of us. John Goodman was always a great host, and having the old-timers on the show was incredible. The reason we were all there was standing next to us at the coffee machine. What I noticed most about Aykroyd and Bill Murray was how much bigger they were than I had anticipated. They were both over six feet tall and looked as if they could hold their own in a bar fight if they had to. I wasn't in any sketches, and I was really disappointed. Nothing would have been cooler than to stand next to Bill Murray or Dan Aykroyd in a sketch.

Two weeks later, I came up with an original character and a sketch titled "Rock and Roll Real Estate." In it, I played a real estate agent who used to be the lead singer of an eighties metal band. I screamed all of my lines at the top of my lungs as if I were onstage in a giant arena. I submitted it in week eighteen when Courteney Cox hosted. I had both "Good Morning, Brooklyn" and "Rock and Roll Real Estate" on the board that week, so I was looking really good. I was hoping that two original characters on one show might take the taste of Rick Shapiro's lawyers out of Lorne's mouth.

But "Rock and Roll Real Estate" was cut after dress rehearsal on Saturday afternoon. In the meeting, I was told by Lorne to make sure I resubmitted it the following week, which I did. Again, it was chosen for air. Bob Saget, an incredibly funny guy, was the host. He also had the most disgusting sense of humor of any human being I've ever met. He would be talking about raping his mother and having sex with his daughter—no, he'd say, I was having sex with someone's else daughter and then I brought her home to have sex with my daughter, but first I took a shit on them.

The only host who came close to Saget's toilet talk was Emilio Estevez, who was easily one of the coolest people I met during my *SNL* years. Every joke Emilio told was about his rosebud (which he taught me meant asshole), but he told them in the funniest way with a real quick wit. I'd ask him what he was doing later and he'd launch into a riff like "I don't know, licking your rosebud. You sleep on your stomach, don't you? Okay, then, I'll be over at ten."

I thought the sketch worked better with Bob than it had with Courteney Cox because Saget was funny playing the straight man to my screaming metal head, but "Rock and Roll Real Estate" was cut again on Saturday after dress rehearsal. Again, Lorne told me to make sure I resubmitted it the following week. I complied and for the third consecutive week, "Rock and Roll Real Estate" was chosen to be on *Saturday Night Live*.

It was the last show of the year and David Duchovny was hosting. Everybody was very loose all week, and the pickup basketball game was particularly competitive that week. Another season was ending. Critically, it had gone much better than my first one. This meant that instead of headlines like "Saturday Night Dead," the *New York Post* now wrote nothing. We all knew the show was funnier than it had been the previous year, and it also seemed that everyone definitely had more fun.

In the "Rock and Roll Real Estate" sketch, I wore a big blond teased-out wig, leather pants, and a Realtor's jacket. My hair looked just like Rod Stewart's hair; Rod Stewart was the musical guest on the twentieth and final show. After I rehearsed "Rock and Roll Real Estate" on Saturday, Rod was scheduled to do his rehearsal immediately after me. He was standing off to the side during my rehearsal. I wanted to stop and tell him that despite how I looked, I wasn't doing an impression of him.

When Rod Stewart finished his rehearsal, he had to walk past me to get back to his dressing room. He was surrounded by about ten people who walked with him and formed a circle as he passed. One of the people in the circle pointed at me and said, "What's up, Rod!" I started to worry that Rod Stewart would have my sketch cut again because I was dancing around like a jackass and screaming while wearing a Rod Stewart wig.

It turned out that Rod Stewart wasn't too concerned with my possible impersonation, and the sketch made it through dress rehearsal and the meeting in Lorne's office and onto the show. It was scheduled last in the rundown, just before Good-nights. I stood on the sidelines of everyone else's sketches and kept checking my watch to make sure the show was running on time. I had to get this sketch on the air. It had already been picked three times, it was original, and it was funny. I knew I had to end the year strong. Finishing up the season with some momentum would help my negotiations over the summer, or so I thought.

But by the time "Rock and Roll Real Estate" aired on *Saturday Night Live,* the sketch had been read at three consecutive read-throughs. It had been rehearsed three times on Thursday or Friday night and three more times on Saturday for camera blocking. It had been performed in three live dress rehearsals in front of three different studio audiences. When David Duchovny, Molly Shannon, and I took our places during the second to last commercial break of the season, the sketch was about to be done out loud for the thirteenth time in three weeks.

The show had run like clockwork and the sketch did not get cut. It bombed horribly, which was made worse by the fact that I was dancing around like a jackass during its demise. Each time the sketch had been cut, I had performed it the next time with a little something extra at the read-throughs and the rehearsals. Twelve times I gave everything I had. My intensity increased incrementally with each performance or rehearsal. When the sketch reached America on the thirteenth try, it got no laughs. The sketch, like me, was tired.

I finished the sketch knowing that it had tanked. I knew the reason it tanked was because I had no more energy. I now hated the sketch. They could have taken it away from me whenever they wanted, which made the actual performing of the sketch more of a fuck-you than the great experience it should have been. When the sketch ended, I pulled my Rod Stewart wig off by myself, ripping out some of my hair that was bobby-pinned to my scalp and the wig. I didn't care. It was over. Once again, I had survived the madness for twenty weeks.

The season-ending after-party was held at the skating rink at 30 Rock, and it was an extravagant affair attended by countless celebrities as well as former hosts and cast members. I actually enjoyed myself at the party and didn't get as drunk as usual. I got home at a decent hour, went straight to bed, and slept until 5:30 P.M. the following day. I woke up to pee and went right back to bed and slept until early Monday morning, at which point I woke up to pack for my afternoon flight back to Los Angeles.

On the flight, I took out a yellow legal pad and began to make another list. This was a list of things that I would have to be assured would change if I was going to return to the show. I was prepared to walk away. If I was going to be on *Saturday Night Live* for a third season, things were going to have to change. Never again, I wrote, would Don Pardo scream, "And featuring!" before he announced my name. If I came back, it was going to be as a full cast member. Never again would I have to sit in an elevator shaft on a show night and scribble caveman drawings on the walls in pencil. Never again would someone write me into a sketch as a guy who says nothing, like some extra they dragged off the street.

Over the summer, I continued to add to my list. I made it abundantly clear to my agent that if I was to return to the show, these changes would have to be implemented. If I remained on *Saturday Night Live,* I had firmly made up my mind that I was going to be treated better, and I didn't care if I had to put it in writing. I wanted more money, not as a reward for the great work I had done, but for standing around and eating shit over the last two seasons. I figured that if the show had more of a financial interest in me, they might choose more of my sketches on Wednesday nights. I went over my plans with my agent, Ruthanne, and my manager, Barry. I was ready for battle.

I learned that summer that you can't fight someone if he doesn't show up.

The show again had a contractual option for my services that they didn't have to activate until July 1. Unlike the previous summer, I didn't worry about the option over my summer vacation. Stealing from Rick Shapiro probably hadn't helped my chances, but the fact that I had come up with James Barone and "Rock and Roll Real Estate" might. I felt that Ricki Lake, Christopher Walken, and Harvey Keitel were icing on the cake. I had not appeared on camera as much as I would have liked, but when I did get on, I showed that I could do an incredibly diverse array of impressions, as well as create some recurring characters. Even "Rock and Roll Real Estate" could be resurrected and saved. I felt confident that the show would call my agent long before the July 1 deadline, but they didn't.

On July 1, the NBC lawyers called my agent. Instead of begging to have me back, they were asking for an extension on the option until July 6, just as they had done the previous year. I told Ruthanne that I wanted an answer now instead of later. Again, she reminded me that it probably wasn't best to push their hand if they were asking for an extension, so again I agreed to the five-day extension. I pacified myself by polishing the complaints on my list.

On July 6, the show called and asked for another extension. This time they told my agent they needed until July 14. Again, I agreed to the extension and the power of my list slowly disintegrated. On July 14, the show called my agent and asked for another extension. They now needed until July 24 to decide if they wanted me back. My lists were useless. Like the previous summer, I had been stripped down naked and made to wait by the phone. Just like last year, I was hoping the phone would ring and praying that I was still welcome on the seventeenth floor of 30 Rock. Then, on July 24, the show called my agent and asked for another extension.

When Ruthanne called me to relay the news, I didn't shout or complain. I didn't ask her advice on how to proceed. I remained calm. I took a breath and told her, using a single word, that I was finished with it all. I told her to go back to the show and tell them that I didn't accept their option. I told her no. She explained to me that by doing so, I might be helping them make their decision. I no longer cared what their decision was. I was done.

This was the biggest professional decision I had ever made, but I was never so sure of anything in my life. It was over. How could I go back? If I decided I wanted to go back, I had a list of demands that I wanted met. But now I was on the fifth extension of the option, and with each extension I had been stripped of negotiating power. I don't know what was said behind closed doors or what considerations were involved in rehiring me. I didn't care. It was over.

I tried for twenty weeks to put a square peg into a round hole. I took a summer off and tried it again for twenty more weeks. I was defeated. I no longer wanted to swim upstream. I was tired of dressing rooms and Marisa Tomei and sketches getting cut after dress rehearsal. I was tired of waiting for Jim Downey to finish watching high school basketball games. I was tired of getting fall-down drunk at the after-parties. I was tired of Rob Schneider looking at sushi through a jeweler's loupe. I was tired of hearing "you can't say *get laid*" at 12:15 A.M. on *Saturday Night Live*. I was tired of complaining, and most of all, I was tired of being a phony.

Like many performers, when I was first hired for *Saturday Night Live,* I had a constant feeling of "What am I doing here?" Now, two years and forty shows later, I was still asking the same question. How bad do I want to go to work for a group of people that need five extensions to decide whether they wanted me back? In regards to *Saturday Night Live,* I would never ask myself that question again. I was empty. I had no fight left in me. They had won. I was tired.

I needed a nap.

PHIL HARTMAN, U.S.A.

WHEN I think back on *Saturday Night Live,* I see the show in a series of snapshots. Three types of shots play out in my head. The first group of photos are very benign. I see the writers' room with all of the chairs in it, the stage in studio 8-H, the hallways and the pictures on the walls, and the corners and the sides of people's faces. I have no emotion when I think of these things. I feel as if someone I don't know is showing me pictures of the inside of their house.

The next set of snapshots always makes me smile. I see Fred Wolf, who does not smoke, walking around with an unlit cigarette in his mouth all night on Tuesdays; Bob Van Rye and Jane the janitor smiling; Jim Downey walking out of his office and brushing his teeth at the same time; Dave Attell in his denim jacket; Adam Sandler, David Spade, and Tim Meadows all laughing at one of Sandler's stories; the couch I sat on my first day; Norm Macdonald smiling and lighting up the room; and Don Pardo ready to tell the world who will be on *Saturday Night Live* that week.

The final group of snapshots I see in my head are more like little short movies. They are snippets of conversations and pieces of sketches that last a few seconds, but linger with me for days. The longer these scenarios repeat in my head, the more they trigger other memories that I had temporarily forgotten. All of these vignettes are special. I enjoy thinking back on them when I am lying in my bed alone at night. One montage ends in a single image that stands out above all others: May 14, 1994, Phil Hartman and Chris Farley's last show.

The final sketch of that show was a musical tribute to Phil, who had received a bronze tube of glue from the cast earlier that day to commemorate the nickname given to him by Sandler. Wearing a double-breasted charcoal suit with a maroon and white polka-dot tie, Phil began the sketch by smiling and addressing the camera: "Ladies and gentlemen, as we close out our nineteenth season, let's say good-bye to the *Saturday Night Live* family singers." Phil waved his hand toward the stage behind him and we all marched out.

The entire cast, as well as all the featured performers, filed onto the stage and began to sing "So Long, Farewell" from the movie *The Sound of Music*. There were fourteen of us onstage, and we were all dressed as our recurring characters. We all belted out: "So long, farewell, auf Wiedersehen good night" and waved good-bye.

Then Adam Sandler and David Spade sang by themselves, as the Gap Girls: "We sell you jeans, like even if they're too tight." Then Sandler and Spade giggled like girls and danced off the stage. That left twelve of us. Some of us waved when we should have squatted. Some of us squatted when we were supposed to wave. The entire thing was very poorly rehearsed.

Next, Melanie Hutsell as Tori Spelling and Tim Meadows as Ike Turner sang to Kevin Nealon, who didn't have any lines in the song. The three of them danced off the stage. Then Norm Macdonald, Sarah Silverman, and I sang, "We're not on a lot, so we better try and score" and we danced off the stage. As we exited, Sarah jumped up on my back and Norm sort of sulked along behind us with his hands in his pockets.

That left seven people on the stage. Mike Myers as Linda Richman from "Coffee Talk" sang his solo and did a hora off the stage, and the crowd went bananas. That was the first applause break of the sketch. Ellen Cleghorne sang as Zoraida the NBC page, and she too received an applause break.

Four people stood on the stage and continued singing "So long, farewell." Rob Schneider as the Copy Guy and Julia Sweeney as Pat sang a duet and left the other cast members standing behind them. Michael McKean was dressed as Lenny from *Laverne & Shirley*. He sang, "I don't have a character yet, but I was on *Laverne & Shirley*." He did his dance off the stage as Lenny, and the crowd applauded along with hoots and hollers.

That left one person onstage. It was Chris Farley dressed as the Motivational Speaker. Before he even opened his mouth, the crowd went apeshit. He started to walk to the front of the stage, hitching his pants up as he walked. At this point in the sketch, the song had slowed down to a lullaby and Chris began singing softly, "So long, farewell, hey, what am I, chopped liver?" He let out a yawn and sat down on the edge of the stage and continued, "I need to sleep in a van down by the river." Chris yawned again and bowed his head as if he had fallen asleep.

Phil Hartman walked out from the side of the stage and sat down next to Chris. As Phil sat, Chris rested his head on Phil's lapel. Phil then looked at the camera again and said, "You know, I can't imagine a more dignified way . . ." That's when his voice cracked. The glue. It was the last thing he was going to say on *Saturday Night Live* as a cast member. The sight of Phil's eyes getting moist was stunning. His voice quivered as if he might cry, and he paused for a second to collect himself. He continued speaking into the camera, saying, "To end my eight years on this program . . ." Chris cuddled up into Phil and Phil sang, "Good-bye. Good-bye. Good-bye." The camera angle on the last "good-bye" switched to the crane camera that swung through the studio. Phil was looking up as he sang. Farley nuzzled in closer to Phil and moved his head from Phil's lapel to his shoulder. The sketch ended like that, with Phil Hartman and Chris Farley sitting onstage together, sleeping and singing "Good-bye."

The stage lights dimmed and the only light left on the stage was a small spot focused on Chris and Phil. The entire stage was dark except for the circle of light on the shoulders and heads of Chris and Phil. When this snapshot comes into my mind, it remains longer than the others. It's as if you were staring into a lightbulb the moment someone switches it off. The room goes dark, but you can still see the coils of the bulb.

Whenever I think of Phil and Chris sitting together on the stage in studio 8-H in the early morning hours of May 15, 1994, to say that it was all worthwhile is belittling. It was glorious.